The Creeper

A Play

Pauline Macaulay

A SAMUEL FRENCH ACTING EDITION

FOUNDED 1830

SAMUELFRENCH-LONDON.CO.UK
SAMUELFRENCH.COM

Copyright © 1965 by Pauline Macaulay
All Rights Reserved

THE CREEPER is fully protected under the copyright laws of the British Commonwealth, including Canada, the United States of America, and all other countries of the Copyright Union. All rights, including professional and amateur stage productions, recitation, lecturing, public reading, motion picture, radio broadcasting, television and the rights of translation into foreign languages are strictly reserved.

ISBN 978-0-573-04010-8

www.samuelfrench-london.co.uk

www.samuelfrench.com

For Amateur Production Enquiries

United Kingdom and World excluding North America

plays@SamuelFrench-London.co.uk

020 7255 4302/01

Each title is subject to availability from Samuel French,

depending upon country of performance.

CAUTION: Professional and amateur producers are hereby warned that THE CREEPER is subject to a licensing fee. Publication of this play does not imply availability for performance. Both amateurs and professionals considering a production are strongly advised to apply to the appropriate agent before starting rehearsals, advertising, or booking a theatre. A licensing fee must be paid whether the title is presented for charity or gain and whether or not admission is charged.

The professional rights in this play are controlled by Samuel French Ltd, 52 Fitzroy Street, London, W1T 5JR.

No one shall make any changes in this title for the purpose of production. No part of this book may be reproduced, stored in a retrieval system, or transmitted in any form, by any means, now known or yet to be invented, including mechanical, electronic, photocopying, recording, videotaping, or otherwise, without the prior written permission of the publisher. No one shall upload this title, or part of this title, to any social media websites.

The right of Pauline Macaulay to be identified as author of this work has been asserted by her in accordance with Section 77 of the Copyright, Designs and Patents Act 1988

THE CREEPER

First produced at the Nottingham Playhouse on the 28th October 1964, and subsequently by Stephen Mitchell at the St Martin's Theatre, London, on the 15th July 1965, with the following cast of characters—

(in the order of their appearance)

HOLMES, the manservant	*George Merritt*
MAURICE	*Peter Blythe*
EDWARD KIMBERLEY	*Eric Portman*
MICHEL	*Noel Davis*
MAN IN A RAINCOAT	*Jonathan Newth*

Directed by DONALD McWHINNIE
Designed by HUTCHINSON SCOTT

SYNOPSIS OF SCENES

The action of the play passes in the lounge of Edward Kimberley's house

ACT I

SCENE 1 Late afternoon
SCENE 2 Two a.m. the following morning

ACT II

SCENE 1 Morning, some weeks later
SCENE 2 Later the same afternoon

ACT III

SCENE 1 Midday, about ten days later
SCENE 2 The evening of the same day

Time—the present

THE CREEPER

ACT I

SCENE I

SCENE—*The lounge of Edward Kimberley's house. Late afternoon. It is a rather beautifully furnished room. A door L leads to the hall and other parts of the house. There are french windows R leading to a terrace with the garden beyond. The fireplace up LC is old and a log fire burns in it. Up R is an alcove lined with books. There is a console table down R with a picture on the wall over it. A small armchair is down R. Another table is R with a mirror on the wall over it. In the alcove there is an occasional chair, a sculpture of a torso and a pedestal with a table-lamp on it. Up R is a period desk with a desk chair. A built-in radio is in the wall over the left end of the desk. A basket of logs stands R of the fireplace. There is a sideboard L with a mirror over it and an occasional chair down L, below the door. An Empire style sofa is C with a stool L of it and a round table R of it. An armchair stands LC with an occasional table L of it. There are heavy velvet curtains at the windows, a large circular carpet on the floor LC and a smaller rectangular carpet on the floor RC. There is a bell-pull R of the fireplace. At night the room is lit by chandeliers pendant up R and down LC, and table-lamps on the table R, on the desk and on the sideboard. The hall off L is furnished with a table with a lamp on it and a picture on the wall.*

When the CURTAIN *rises the room is empty. There is a log fire burning in the grate.* HOLMES, *the manservant, enters from the hall and stands aside.* MAURICE *follows him on.* HOLMES *is old and very bent.* MAURICE *is a young man of twenty-five.* HOLMES *exits* L, *closing the door behind him.* MAURICE *sits on the sofa and looks around him. He seems slightly ill at ease. After a few seconds his eyes fall on a letter lying on the floor* LC. *He rises, goes to the letter and looks down at it. He hesitates and then leaves it where it is, after first walking round it and trying to read it without picking it up. He then moves up* R *and looks in a mirror on the wall over a table* R. *He adjusts his tie and the stiff collar of his clean, white, rather too stiff shirt, steps a few paces backwards and then forwards again. His eyes alight on a bowl of fruit on the table down* R *and he moves to it. He looks about him then lifts a bunch of grapes, pulls off several from underneath, crams them into his mouth then quickly replaces the bunch, plucked side downwards. He turns and his eyes fall on an appetizing plate of petit-fours on the table* RC. *He goes to the table, looks about, then eats two petit-fours and rearranges the remainder. He crosses to* LC *and his eyes fall again on*

1

the letter on the floor. *He looks about him and then picks up the letter and reads it. His reaction is puzzled and he replaces the letter on the floor. He walks aimlessly about and looks at his watch. He sees a little silver box on the occasional table* LC, *goes to it and casually lifts the lid. He gasps. Silently, from the french window behind him, steps* EDWARD KIMBERLEY. EDWARD *is aged fifty.*

EDWARD. It's not a human eye—it's a dog's.

(MAURICE *closes the lid with a start and turns*)

(*He crosses to* C) A very good hunting dog of mine, actually. I was very fond of him. I used to like the way he looked at me, so when he died . . . (*He gestures*) It's in pickle. (*He smiles*) I take it you've come in answer to my advertisement.

MAURICE. Y-yes.

EDWARD (*indicating the sofa*) Do sit down.

(MAURICE *moves to the sofa and sits on the edge of it*)

(*He moves to* L *of Maurice and proffers a gold cigarette case*) Cigarette?

(MAURICE *takes a cigarette rather nervously*)

(*He lights Maurice's cigarette with a gold lighter*) Your name is . . . ?

MAURICE. Morris.

EDWARD. Maurice?

MAURICE. Maurice Morris.

EDWARD. Maurice Maurice? Oh, Maurice Morris. Really? How delightful.

(MAURICE *visibly brightens*)

(*He bends down, picks up the letter and waves it*) What did you think of it?

MAURICE (*reddening*) Oh, er—well, I thought it had been dropped accidentally, sir—so I picked it up and . . .

EDWARD. Put it back again—of course. What did you think of it?

MAURICE (*hesitantly*) I . . .

EDWARD. Never mind—(*he tears the letter into little pieces and throws them into the fire*) it's quite fictitious. And I wouldn't blame you if you didn't understand it because it was written to a dog. (*He pauses and sits in the armchair* LC) Well, Maurice Morris—apart from your name, I only know two things about you—you are hungry and curious in that order. Shall we find out a little more?

MAURICE (*pulling out an envelope*) I've got some references, sir.

EDWARD (*waving the envelope aside*) No. No. Don't mean a thing—anybody can write them. What was your last job?

MAURICE (*after the slightest hesitation*) Austin Reed's, sir.

EDWARD. I know the name. What did you do for them?

MAURICE. I sold shirts and—er—ties, sir.

EDWARD. Did you? (*He pulls down the cuffs of his shirt and lifts his chin*) What size collar do you think I take? (*He waves a hand*) From where you are.
MAURICE (*after a slight pause; hopefully*) Fifteen? And a half?
EDWARD (*smiling*) Splendid. Well, you know about necks. (*He crosses his legs and shows an expanse of mauve silk sock*) Do you like these socks?
MAURICE. Yes, they're very nice.
EDWARD. I think so. (*He uncrosses his legs*) I'm glad you like the colour—it would be rather unfortunate if you didn't because it's all over the house—well, in the bedrooms, anyway. (*He stares hard at Maurice*)

(MAURICE *begins to look rather awkward*)

You're not happy in that collar, are you?
MAURICE. Not very, sir.
EDWARD. Then why do you wear it? I suppose you thought it was expected of you. Never do that—if you don't like stiff collars, don't try to look like a man who does. If you do, it means that you are trying to sell an impression of yourself which is not you at all. Do you follow me?
MAURICE. Yes, sir.
EDWARD. Loosen it.
MAURICE. Yes, sir. (*He loosens his tie and breathes more freely*) Thank you, sir.
EDWARD. How old are you, Maurice?
MAURICE. Twenty-five, sir.
EDWARD (*rising*) I'm fifty—exactly twice your age. (*He looks at Maurice for a moment then moves to the fire, looks into it and holds out a hand to warm it*)

(MAURICE *sits in uncomfortable silence*)

(*After a few seconds he lifts his head and turns to Maurice*) You can't possibly have any conception of what it's like to be fifty. (*He pauses*) Why did you answer my advertisement? I usually get ex male nurses from mental hospitals.
MAURICE. I wanted to do something different, sir.
EDWARD. Yes—most people do. I hope you've given it some thought. Companion to an eccentric can cover a lot of things, you know.
MAURICE. Yes, sir. I realize that.
EDWARD. Am I what you expected?

(MAURICE *hesitates*)

Perhaps you imagined I would be in my dotage—slightly senile—not very aware of what's going on?
MAURICE. Well, I didn't know really, sir—what . . .

EDWARD. You'd find—quite. (*He pauses briefly*) You smoke—do you drink?
MAURICE. Moderately, sir.
EDWARD. How very dull. You're trying to create an impression again—of respectability. I'm not interested in respectability. Let's start again—do you drink?
MAURICE. Yes, sir.
EDWARD. Ever in excess?
MAURICE. Sometimes, sir.
EDWARD. Splendid! Now. (*He thinks*) You have a good appetite—yes? Do you have good health?
MAURICE. Yes, sir.
EDWARD. You are fortunate. What are your sexual habits?

(MAURICE *starts*)

Never mind—if you live here I'll find out. Would you like some tea? (*He pulls the bell-pull* R *of the fireplace, then moves to the small built-in radio in the wall up* RC *and switches it on*)

(*Ballet music is heard from the radio.* EDWARD *makes ballet gestures with his hands. He looks lonely and sad. After a few seconds he switches the radio off*)

(*He smiles at Maurice*) Too nostalgic. (*He moves* LC)

(MAURICE *nods*.
    MICHEL *enters from the hall and looks enquiringly at Edward.*
MICHEL *is a tall, thin, rather beautiful young man of twenty-seven. He wears sweater and jeans*)

Michel. I sent Holmes off. Do you think you could bring us some tea?
MICHEL (*rather sullenly*) Very well. Black or white?
EDWARD (*to Maurice*) Black or white tea?
MAURICE. Oh—er—white, please.
EDWARD (*to Maurice*) Allow me to introduce you. This is Michel—whose job you will be taking if I find you suitable.

(MAURICE *starts to rise*)

(*To Michel*) Michel—this is Maurice—(*he pauses briefly*) Maurice.
MICHEL (*to Maurice; rudely*) I wish you luck, I must say.

(MICHEL *exits to the hall, slamming the door behind him.* MAURICE *drops back on to the sofa*)

EDWARD. He's a bit touchy just now. Nice looking, isn't he?
MAURICE. Er . . . (*Brightly*) Yes.
EDWARD. He's rather narcissistic about it. Actually his name isn't 'Michel', it's 'Michael'. I just decided to call him 'Michel' when he came here. On the day he leaves I shall call him 'Michael'. 'Good-bye, Michael,' I shall say—'good-bye.' I like

your name, Maurice, it's rather appealing. As a matter of fact, it's one of the few things in your favour. You don't give a very good impression, actually—you sit there and you say—'Yes', and 'er' and 'oh'—and that's about all.

MAURICE. I'm sorry.

EDWARD (*sitting in the armchair* LC) So am I. However, it looks as if I'll have to make the best of it. Sad to relate, you are the only person who answered my advertisement. I think a lot of them were put off by the word 'eccentric'. It's a strange thing, you know, but many people seem to be under the impression that 'eccentric' is a polite way of saying 'a bit gone'—that's slightly eccentric, of course—and 'very eccentric' means 'mad as a hatter'. It just isn't true. Have you ever been inside a lunatic asylum? As a visitor, of course. Well, I have, and I can tell you that the real lunatics aren't eccentric at all. On the contrary, they give the impression of being extraordinarily sane—too sane, if you know what I mean. Why do you want to work for me?

MAURICE. To be truthful, sir, I was fed up.

EDWARD. With shirts and ties? I suppose you would be. No underwear?

MAURICE. No, sir.

EDWARD. What do you think of these fish-net vests that seem to be the rage?

MAURICE. Well, it's a matter of taste, sir.

EDWARD. Yes. Not mine. I like silk next to my skin. (*He pauses briefly*) I suppose the part you liked best in my advertisement was the bit about 'excellent remuneration for the right man'?

MAURICE. Well, I won't deny I was interested in the money, sir. Could you tell me how much it is exactly?

EDWARD. Certainly. Thirty shillings per week.

MAURICE (*his face falling*) A—week?

EDWARD. Five shillings extra if you drive a car. Do you?

MAURICE. Er . . .

EDWARD. Do you drive a car?

MAURICE. I have done, sir.

EDWARD (*pained*) Have done?

MAURICE. What I mean is, sir, I haven't got a car of my own.

EDWARD. Yes, I understand. Ever killed anybody?

MAURICE. No, sir.

EDWARD. Ever knocked anybody down?

MAURICE. No, sir.

EDWARD. Ever driven a car under the influence of drink?

MAURICE (*emphatically*) No, sir.

EDWARD. Well, you'll have to learn how to do that if you're going to be of any use to me.

MAURICE. Y-yes, sir.

EDWARD (*after a slight pause*) Now—where were we? Oh, yes. Thirty-five shillings a week. I suppose you think that's not very much. However, you will get full board—excellent meals—followed by brandy and cigars. In between snacks—alcoholic drinks and cigarettes. I will also buy your clothes—everything down to your... (*He smiles*) You see, I want you to be dependent upon me. I don't want you opening a savings account behind my back—you know the sort of thing people do. I want you to feel you are living with me because you like living with me—not as a sort of 'get rich quick scheme'—you know what I mean? Actually, if we get on, you can have more or less anything you desire. The only thing is, that should you decide to leave—*it* stays here. Do you understand me?

MAURICE. Yes. (*He rises*) I don't think I'm the right person.

EDWARD (*without moving*) I'm the one who advertised—let me be the judge of that.

MAURICE. No—er—thank you very much, but I don't think... (*Firmly*) I made a mistake.

EDWARD. Did you?

MAURICE. Yes. I'm not suitable. (*He edges towards the door*)

EDWARD (*without getting up*) Maurice Morris, please don't go. You see, I'm afraid you're thinking conventionally—remember I'm an eccentric.

MAURICE (*embarrassed*) No, but I mean—it seems perfectly clear that...

EDWARD. That I'm an old queen? I'm not, actually. Nor am I anything else. I lost interest in sex many years ago in the physical sense—aesthetically I find it quite interesting—the performance bores me. It's much more exciting in my head, if you know what I mean.

MAURICE (*quite keenly*) Yes—yes, I do.

EDWARD. So you've nothing to worry about. The most I shall expect from you if I can't sleep—is a game of cards. Can you play gin-rummy?

MAURICE. Yes, sir.

EDWARD. Good.

(*There is a slight pause*)

(*He rises*) Come and have a look at my garden. (*He crosses to the french windows*)

(MAURICE *joins Edward at the french windows*)

Rather beautiful, isn't it? (*He points into the garden*) Do you think I should have that tree cut down? I suppose it's rather dangerous, but I find it fascinating. The creeper on it is so beautiful, yet it has killed the tree. It's so wonderfully gnarled and twisted, if you look at it long enough, you can read anything you want in it.

MAURICE. It's like a painting I once saw.

(*There is a pause.*

MICHEL *enters from the hall with a clatter of crockery. He carries a tray of tea for three. He raises his eyebrows slightly at the backs of Edward and Maurice*)

EDWARD (*turning*) Ah—tea.

(MICHEL *arranges the tea on the table* RC. EDWARD *leads* MAURICE LC)

Are you going to join us, Michel?
MICHEL. If I must.
EDWARD. You were going to, anyway—you brought three cups. (*Aside to Maurice*) He's frightened of missing something. (*Louder*) Would you like to sit here? (*He indicates the sofa*)

(MAURICE *sits on the sofa*)

(*He sits in the armchair* LC) Michel will pour.

(MICHEL *rather sullenly pours out the tea and hands it round*)

(*To Maurice*) He's rather nice when he smiles. I must confess it's hard to tell at the moment. (*To Michel*) The man didn't come to tune the piano—do you know why?
MICHEL. I rang him up.
EDWARD. Well, see about it again in the morning.

(MICHEL *sighs*)

(*To Maurice*) Do you play?
MAURICE. Not really. Only that . . . (*He breaks off*)
EDWARD (*politely*) Yes?
MAURICE. Well, that piece for two hands.

(MICHEL *raises his eyebrows*)

It goes—(*to the tune of 'Oh, Mother, Hang the Washing Out Across the Village Green'*) Dah didah didah didah di. Dah didahdidahdi. Dahdidahdidahdidahdidahdidahdidahdi.
EDWARD. I don't think I know it. Anyway, it doesn't matter. *I* play—all I require is that *you* listen.
MAURICE. Oh, I like listening to music. I like that very much.
EDWARD. Good. I shall look forward to playing to you. Michel here is a very bad listener—he has no ear for music at all.
MICHEL. I don't care—I really don't. (*He sits on the chair down* L)
EDWARD. Just because you're under notice, you don't have to be so bad-tempered. (*To Maurice*) He's piqued because I won't let him take his suits away with him when he goes. There's one in green antelope that he's particularly keen on.
MICHEL. My clothes were part of my salary.
EDWARD (*to Maurice*) I explained everything to him about that —when he came here—just like I have to you. I thought it was quite clear—but no—he wants to have his cake and eat it.
MICHEL (*sulkily*) They won't fit him, he's smaller than me.

EDWARD. That is quite irrelevant. He's a new employee—he gets new clothes. I don't expect him to wear cast-offs.
MICHEL. So why can't I . . . ?
MAURICE (*not quite understanding*) Look—I really don't mind—it doesn't matter at all. Anyway, I don't know if . . .
EDWARD. That's very nice of you, but I wouldn't think of it. No man can wear another man's clothes—it never looks right.
MAURICE. No, well, as I said, sir, I haven't . . .
EDWARD. Made up your mind about staying? I do hope you'll say 'yes'. You see, Michel and I are getting on each other's nerves.
MICHEL. It isn't my fault.
EDWARD. We won't go into that. (*To Maurice*) What about some more tea?
MAURICE. Thank you very much.
EDWARD. Michel?
MICHEL. If he's going to work here he'll have to pour his own tea.
MAURICE. Oh, I'm sorry. (*He rises*)
EDWARD (*waving him down*) Please.

(MAURICE *resumes his seat*)

Michel—I know this job has been a great disappointment to you. I sympathize—but until you do actually leave—kindly fulfil your duties.

(MICHEL, *with bad grace, rises, pours another cup of tea for Maurice then resumes his seat*)

(*To Maurice*) Michel, you see, is one of those who looked upon me as a 'get rich quick scheme'.
MICHEL (*to Maurice*) It's all lies.
EDWARD. Michel, you know, is like the creeper on the tree in the garden. He has to be cut away before he destroys the sap. (*He looks at his watch*) It's time for my rest. (*He rises. To Maurice*) I usually lie down about this time. Are you in a very great hurry?
MAURICE (*rising*) No, sir.
EDWARD. What I mean is, have you any appointments?
MAURICE. No, sir.
EDWARD. Will you stay for dinner?
MAURICE. Thank you, sir.
EDWARD. By then you should have had ample leisure to decide whether you would like to live here. (*He takes Maurice's hand for a moment*) I should be very happy if you would. (*He crosses to the hall door and turns*) Michel will show you around the house. He will also give you a lot of information—most of which I should ignore.

(EDWARD *exits to the hall.* MAURICE *resumes his seat and picks up his cup of tea. He does not know what to say.* MICHEL *rises, crosses to the table* R, *takes a cigarette from the box on it and slams down the* lid. *He lights the cigarette, using a match from the box on the table, then goes to the french windows and gazes out.* MAURICE *empties his cup, rises, puts his cup on the tray and clears his throat*)

MAURICE. Er—excuse me, but how long have you been working here?
MICHEL (*turning his head very slowly*) What?
MAURICE. How long have you been working here?
MICHEL. Six months, and I'm a nervous wreck. (*He turns back and blows smoke up at the ceiling*)
MAURICE. Oh. (*He pauses*) Is it—very . . . ?
MICHEL (*with a gesture*) What about that garden?
MAURICE. Yes, it's . . .
MICHEL. Nature gone mad. (*He turns*) What were you going to say?
MAURICE (*tentatively*) I quite like wild gardens.
MICHEL. Oh, well—(*he gestures*) it's all yours. (*He goes to the table down* R *and lifts the grapes from the fruit bowl. He is about to take some when he sees some have been picked from underneath*) Did you take those?

(MAURICE *looks discomfited*)

I call that very sly of you.
MAURICE (*rather crimson*) I'm sorry.
MICHEL (*replacing the grapes*) Don't mention it—I couldn't care less, really. (*He crosses to the armchair* LC *and flings himself into it*) I'm so bored. I've never been so bored in my life.
MAURICE (*nervously*) Yes. (*He sits on the sofa*) Er—do you think you could tell me, please—what my work here—what exactly would I have to do?
MICHEL. Oh, really! I don't see why I should have to explain all that.
MAURICE. No—but if you could just tell me . . .
MICHEL. Just what it says—be a companion.
MAURICE. You mean—talk to him and so on?
MICHEL. He talks, you listen. What I've seen of you, you could do that with your eyes shut.
MAURICE. And the piano?
MICHEL. The piano—oh, yes—he told you about that, didn't he—but he didn't tell you when he played. (*He pauses briefly*) He plays—from midnight to two a.m. every night, Sundays included.
MAURICE (*rather taken aback*) Oh.
MICHEL. Then there's gin-rummy at four a.m.
MAURICE. Oh.
MICHEL. Seven a.m. a long walk. Breakfast at eight—and you've got to eat it.
MAURICE. When does he sleep, then?
MICHEL. Sleep? He doesn't sleep.

MAURICE. He must get very tired.
MICHEL. No, you get tired.
MAURICE (*after a slight pause*) What about the daytime?
MICHEL. Depends entirely on his mood. You never know what's going to be in store for you. Drive him into the country for the day to look at some boring old ruins—or stay at home and paint the lavatories black.
MAURICE. Would I have to do any cooking?
MICHEL. Oh, no—nothing like that. He's got a cook daily—and he's got this old manservant Holmes. He's about eighty-two—pretty doddery on his feet—but eyes like a hawk, dear, so watch him. Of course, if he's got the afternoon off, you might have to make the tea.
MAURICE. I wouldn't mind that. I used to make the tea at work, sometimes.
MICHEL. What *was* your work?
MAURICE. Salesman. Shirts and ties.
MICHEL. Really. Where?
MAURICE. Er—Austin Reed's.
MICHEL (*pained*) Oh.
MAURICE. They're a very old firm.
MICHEL. Mm! I go to a little place in Soho—Guys—do you know it?
MAURICE. No, I don't.
MICHEL. They really do have the most dreamy things.
MAURICE. Is that where Mr Kimberley goes?
MICHEL. Oh, no. He has his own tailor in Savile Row. (*He pauses, rises, crosses and sits L of Maurice on the sofa*) Don't you think it's terribly mean of him to make me leave all my clothes behind?
MAURICE. Didn't he explain it all to you in the beginning, then?
MICHEL. Well, he said something—but really! I didn't dream he was serious. For two pins when I do leave, I'll walk out stark naked and get on a bus or something. Then when they pick me up, I shall tell them—I shall say, 'the clothes I came here in wore out'. (*He rises and crosses to* RC) I shall make a little fire of them, you see, before I leave. 'The clothes I came here in wore out and he, Mr Edward Kimberley, refused to give me the others.' 'Thirty bob a week and no clothes,' I shall say. It'd make a lovely scandal. (*He pauses briefly*) You don't seem to find it amusing?
MAURICE. No. You see, I would never dare to do a thing like that—to get on a bus like that.
MICHEL. I'm not sure I'd have the nerve, really. (*He picks up the plate of petit-fours from the table* RC *and offers them to Maurice*)

(MAURICE *shakes his head*)

I suppose you've already had some. (*He eats several petit-fours and replaces the plate on the table* RC) I might as well make the most of them. After all, I don't know where the next meal is coming from.

MAURICE. Look—I don't want to take your job.

MICHEL. It doesn't matter. (*He looks very sad, turns away and takes a handkerchief from his pocket*)

MAURICE (*rising*) Look—please. I'm terribly sorry. I didn't know. I wouldn't dream of coming to work here if . . .

(MICHEL *turns. He is laughing*)

MICHEL (*pointing*) Caught you!

(MAURICE *smiles shyly*)

(*He moves to Maurice and takes him by the hand*) Here. (*He drags Maurice to the occasional table* LC) I've got something to show you. Close your eyes and put your hand out. (*He opens the lid of the eye box*)

MAURICE (*pulling his hand away*) No! I've—I've already seen it.

MICHEL. Oh—pity! You've seen everything. Can you imagine somebody buying you something and then saying you can't have it. I've got a transistor upstairs—sweet—(*he gestures*) that size. I've got to leave it here. I've never worked for anyone so mean—never. (*He moves to the radio in the wall, switches it on and fiddles about with it until he gets some rather hot jazz. He turns it up loud*)

(*After a second or two there is a knocking from above*)

(*He turns up the volume, dances over to Maurice and stands in front of him*) Dance with me?

(*The light begins to dim a little as dusk falls*)

MAURICE. Er—no, I . . .
MICHEL. Oh, go on.
MAURICE. No. No, thank you very much.

(MICHEL *shrugs and dances by himself. He is very light on his feet.*
EDWARD *enters from the hall. He wears a blue silk dressing-gown. He crosses to the radio and abruptly switches it off.* MICHEL *stops dancing*)

EDWARD (*to Michel*) Leave at once!

(MICHEL *stares at Edward*)

Go out of this room and straight out of the front door. Exactly as you came. Don't bother to go upstairs. (*He crosses to the hall door, holds it open and looks at Michel*)

(MICHEL *crosses and exits to the hall*. EDWARD *watches. The front door is heard to slam*)

(*He moves to* L *of Maurice*) I abominate that kind of music. Maurice, are you prepared to live here with me?

MAURICE (*after the faintest hesitation*) Yes, sir.
EDWARD (*smiling*) Would you stay now, leave everything else behind you?
MAURICE (*after the faintest hesitation*) All right, sir.
EDWARD. Thank you. My manservant, Holmes, will prepare your room this evening. Will you forgive me if I return to my rest? Make yourself at home.
MAURICE. Thank you, sir.

(EDWARD *goes to the door and turns*)

EDWARD. My name is 'Edward'.

EDWARD *exits to the hall.* MAURICE *turns, crosses to the french windows and looks out into the falling dusk as—*

the LIGHTS BLACK-OUT

SCENE 2

SCENE—*The same. Two a.m. the following morning.*

When the LIGHTS *come up, the window curtains are closed and the chandeliers are on. We can hear the sound of a rather beautiful classical piece of music being played on a piano in another room.* HOLMES *is arranging a tray with two glasses of hot milk, a bottle of old brandy and two brandy glasses. He puts the tray on the stool in front of the sofa, then goes to the fireplace and stacks the fire with logs. He is very bent in the back and it takes him a little time to lift the logs and put them on the fire. The music comes to an end and after a few seconds* EDWARD *enters from the hall.* MAURICE *follows him on.*

EDWARD. Holmes—Maurice will do that.
MAURICE (*stepping forward*) Yes, I . . .
EDWARD (*to Holmes*) You're an old man, you must go to bed.

(HOLMES *grasps the last log firmly and puts it on to the fire as* MAURICE *moves towards him*)

HOLMES (*turning*) My father was an old man, sir.

(EDWARD *seems to understand this remark*)

EDWARD. Yes, yes, of course. (*He smiles*) So was mine.
HOLMES (*moving to the hall door*) Good night, sir. (*He ignores Maurice*)
EDWARD. Good night, Holmes.

(HOLMES *exits to the hall*)

(*He turns to Maurice*) I must explain that Holmes didn't mean to be rude. You see, there have been a succession of young men here over a period of years—all of whom Holmes disapproved of strongly. After a time he began to behave as if they weren't there —and now—I believe he really doesn't know when they've changed. (*He smiles*) Holmes used to work for my father. He's the last of a dying race. Manservants in the sense of Holmes don't exist any more and never will again. He is, like me, part of a dead world. (*He pauses*) I am surprised you want to enter it.

(*They look at each other and there is a flash of understanding*)
Let us have our night-cap. (*He motions Maurice to sit*)

(MAURICE *sits on the sofa*)

(*He flexes his fingers*) You know, my fingers seem to be getting rather stiff just lately.

MAURICE. Perhaps it's playing the piano too much, sir.
EDWARD (*sharply*) What do you mean?
MAURICE. Nothing. I just thought perhaps . . .
EDWARD. Are you trying to tell me that I shouldn't play the piano?
MAURICE. No . . .
EDWARD (*flexing his fingers; calmer*) I think it's rheumatism. (*He pours two glasses of brandy*)
MAURICE. I've never heard anyone play like you do, sir. It was like going to the Albert Hall.
EDWARD (*a trifle sardonically*) Thank you very much. You have a great feeling for music. I can tell. It's a pity you don't play— very satisfactorily. Would you like to have lessons?
MAURICE. Wouldn't it be too late?
EDWARD. Perhaps. Perhaps not. Anyway, I shall arrange it.

(*He takes a glass of milk and puts it on the table* LC, *then picks up a glass of brandy*)

MAURICE. Thank you. Thank you very much.

(EDWARD *sits in the armchair* LC *and swirls the brandy slowly in his glass*)

EDWARD. My mother was a concert pianist. She began to give me lessons when I was three years old. By the time I was eleven, I had decided to be a concert pianist, too. When I was twelve, my mother left my father for another man. (*He pauses briefly*) I can still remember her perfume, the night she came into my room to say good-bye. She said she was going abroad, to another country, and she would send for me. She told me it was a big secret. Little boys of twelve, then, were not as they are now. She died, I believe, somewhere in Germany during the war. The day after she left, early at practice, my father brought the piano lid down on my fingers. Music was never heard again in this house until my father died. I was thirty, then, and the piano was mine. But my touch was never the same. (*He pauses and sips his brandy*) What did you think of Michel?

MAURICE (*with a slight hesitation*) He's very funny, isn't he?
EDWARD. Funny? Yes, I suppose I found him funny when he first came here. Actually, he isn't funny at all. (*He pauses*) The day he came for his interview, he begged me to take him. He said he was lonely and unhappy and was prepared to do anything. Somehow I found I couldn't refuse. Oh, yes, Michel can be infinitely charming, particularly when he thinks he's on to a good thing. (*He pauses*) Do you think I was too hard on him? Telling him to go like that? I suppose I should have given him some of his things.
MAURICE. Well, sir, I think it was wrong of him to play the music, if he knew you didn't like it.
EDWARD. Yes. You know, Maurice, when you've been here some time, you will find the temptation to do something I don't like is pretty strong.
MAURICE. Yes, sir.
EDWARD. 'Edward.'
MAURICE. Edward.

(EDWARD *drinks some of his milk and* MAURICE *follows suit*)

EDWARD. Maurice, I don't want to be too hard on you the first night.
MAURICE (*sitting more upright*) I'm not at all tired, sir.
EDWARD. Really?
MAURICE. No, sir. Not at all.
EDWARD. How refreshing. Do you suffer from insomnia, too?
MAURICE. A little, sir.
EDWARD. When my mother left us, my father hardly slept at all. He used to get me up in the middle of the night, to play cards with him. I had to play until I fell off the chair. Then they put me back to bed. Holmes and my father. Holmes never used to go to sleep, either—but I think I know Holmes's secret—he was actually asleep all day. Of course, he looked as if he was awake, he went around the house doing the jobs he'd done all his life, but he was really asleep. My father went one better—he walked around dead. (*He smiles*)

(MAURICE *half smiles*)

Maurice, do you have a father?
MAURICE. He died last year, sir.
EDWARD. A mother?
MAURICE. I don't know, sir.
EDWARD. What do you mean—you don't know?
MAURICE. She just went. She just walked out of the house.
EDWARD. We have something in common. (*He pauses*) What was your father's profession?
MAURICE. Salesman, sir.
EDWARD. And your grandfather?

MAURICE. Salesman, sir.
EDWARD (*smiling*) You're stepping out of line.
MAURICE. Yes, sir.

(*There is a pause.* EDWARD *finishes his brandy*)

EDWARD. You aren't drinking your brandy. It's a very old one. Don't you like it?

(MAURICE *quickly picks up his glass and drinks*)

MAURICE. Oh, yes, it's excellent, sir.
EDWARD. 'Edward.'
MAURICE. Edward.
EDWARD (*exasperated*) Maurice Morris—you really are the most incredibly stiff young man I have ever met in my life. I thought at first it was just your collar, but I've now realized it's you. You are completely and utterly stiff all over. I don't think you've ever relaxed in your life. (*He pauses*) Is it something to do with coming from a long line of salesmen?
MAURICE (*looking hopelessly miserable*) I don't know.
EDWARD. Do you *feel* stiff?
MAURICE (*miserably*) Yes, sir.
EDWARD (*shouting*) 'Edward.'
MAURICE (*near to tears*) Yes, Edward.

(EDWARD *rises*)

EDWARD. Look, sit in this chair.

(MAURICE *rises, crosses and sits in the armchair* LC)

Let yourself go limp. Go on! Slouch in the chair.

(MAURICE *slumps down slightly*)

Stick your feet out.

(MAURICE *sticks his feet out*)

Put your arms over the side of the chair.

(MAURICE *puts his arms over the sides of the chair*)

Dangle your hands.

(MAURICE *dangles his hands*)

Now, loosen up your head. (*He wiggles Maurice's head from side to side and up and down*) Now, let your chin drop to your chest.

(MAURICE'S *chin drops to his chest and he closes his eyes*)

Stay like that for a few minutes. (*He picks up his milk and sits on the chair down* L. *After a pause*) How does it feel? (*He pauses*) Rather pleasant, isn't it? You know, I think it's a very bad thing to be tense all the time. One must relax completely for several minutes of every day. (*He pauses*) Maurice? (*He pauses. Louder*) Maurice? (*He rises, bends over Maurice and sees he is asleep*) Ah, well (*He takes his milk to the desk, puts down the glass, switches on the desk lamp, sits at the desk, puts on his spectacles, looks at some correspondence, then commences to write*)

(MAURICE *rises. His eyes are open but he is not awake.* EDWARD *stops writing and looks at Maurice.* MAURICE *takes a balloon from his pocket. He blows it up. It is red and has a rudimentary face painted on it. Simply dots for eyes and nose and a line for the mouth. He looks at the balloon then takes a piece of string from his pocket and ties it round the balloon. He holds one end of the string and lets the balloon float in the air.* EDWARD *watches with amazement.* MAURICE *then moves the chair down* L *to* LC *and ties the balloon to the back of it. He removes his jacket and then his tie. He puts the jacket around the back of the chair, leaving the balloon protruding from the neck. He puts the tie round and ties it neatly. He stands back and regards it. He looks for a moment and then fastens one button of the jacket. The whole arrangement on the chair gives the semblance of a person.* MAURICE *stands back and smiles. He walks around the chair giving the balloon head a little tap so it bobs about. He regards what he has made*)

(*He rises. Softly*) Maurice.

(MAURICE *is still staring at the thing but as Edward speaks an expression of alarm crosses his face. He approaches the shape very slowly, almost stealthily. He takes the ends of the tie in his hands and begins to tighten it.* EDWARD *takes a step forward but stops again. He does not want to disturb the sleeping Maurice.* MAURICE'S *pulling of the tie becomes more and more frenzied. Suddenly the balloon bursts.* MAURICE *is still and silent for a second and then begins to cry. He puts his arms around the shape on the chair and sobs*)

(*He looks very upset, goes quietly to Maurice and puts a hand on his arm. Quietly*) Maurice, you must get dressed.

(MAURICE *stands unseeing.* EDWARD *hurriedly undoes the jacket and manages to pull the tie undone. He puts the tie round Maurice's neck but leaves it loose, then helps him into his jacket, and leads him to the armchair* LC)

Maurice, you must sit down again.

(MAURICE *sits in the armchair*)

(*Softly*) Lie back, Maurice.

(MAURICE *lies back*)

Relax—just relax. (*Very soothingly*) Close your eyes, Maurice.

(MAURICE *closes his eyes and they remain closed.*
EDWARD *unties the burst balloon and throws it in the fire, replaces*

the chair down L and exits to the hall. *He re-enters immediately with a tartan rug which he tucks around Maurice. He stands looking thoughtfully down at him for a moment or two, goes to the desk, switches off the lamp, then goes to the door, switches off the chandeliers and exits to the hall. There is a pause then the window curtains are pulled aside a little.*

MICHEL *peers into the room through the gap in the curtains, then enters, tiptoes to the sideboard* L, *switches on the lamp on it and bends over Maurice)*

MICHEL. Maurice. Maurice.

(MAURICE *opens his eyes and sits up*)

Good morning.

(*There is a slight pause*)

MAURICE (*in a stupor*) Michel. (*He looks around*) What time is it?
MICHEL. Well, it's the middle of the night, really.
MAURICE (*looking around*) Where's . . . ?
MICHEL. Edward's gone to bed. I was watching through the window. (*He crosses and takes a cigarette from the box on the table* R) Did he tuck you up in that rug? How sweet!

(MAURICE *looks down at the rug round his knees*)

(*He lights his cigarette*) Sweet.

(MAURICE *rises quickly and folds the rug*)

(*He crosses to the sideboard, gets a brandy glass, returns* C *and pours a brandy for himself*) I'm so cold, I can't tell you.

(MAURICE *stares at Michel*)

I've been in that terrible garden with that mad creeper for hours.
MAURICE. Why? (*He puts the rug on the chair down* L)
MICHEL. I wanted my transistor. (*He sips his brandy*)
MAURICE. How did you get in?
MICHEL. Is it in your room?
MAURICE. What?
MICHEL. My transistor.
MAURICE. Well—(*he hesitates*) there is one by the bed.
MICHEL. What colour?
MAURICE. Red.
MICHEL. Red? He must have painted it—mine was green.
MAURICE (*seriously*) No, he couldn't have done that. If it was green and he tried to paint it red, it would be blue.

(MICHEL *gives Maurice a pained look*)

MICHEL. Fancy! Well, it must be mine—he hasn't had time to buy another. Can I creep up and get it?

(MAURICE *looks at Michel in amazement*)

Or better still, you go and get it. I might meet Holmes on the landing. (*Entreatingly*) Please, Maurice.
MAURICE. No.
MICHEL. Why not? It belongs to me.
MAURICE (*embarrassed*) No—I can't—do that.
MICHEL. I've got nothing—nothing at all in the world. No job—no money—no clothes—no food.
MAURICE. Look—I'm terribly sorry. I didn't want to take your job—I told you this afternoon. But you said you didn't care, you said you were going anyway.
MICHEL. Pride—that's all it was—pride. And I lost that in the garden.

(*There is a pause.* MAURICE *takes his wallet from his pocket and looks in it*)

MAURICE. I—I could let you have a pound.
MICHEL (*turning his back*) I've never been so insulted.

(MAURICE *slowly replaces the wallet in his pocket then moves to Michel by the stool* C *and nervously touches him on the shoulder*)

MAURICE. I'm sorry, Michel. I didn't mean to offend you.

(*There is a slight pause.* MAURICE *removes his hand*)

MICHEL (*turning*) Do you know what I thought about in that garden?

(MAURICE *shakes his head slightly*)

A hundred and one ways to commit suicide.
MAURICE. Oh.
MICHEL. I suppose you think that's terrible.
MAURICE. No, I don't. We didn't ask to be born—I don't see why we shouldn't be allowed to choose when we die.
MICHEL. Exactly. Maurice, have you ever tried it?
MAURICE. Yes, I did once.
MICHEL. Really? How fascinating. What did you do? How did you go about it?
MAURICE. I took a lot of aspirins.
MICHEL (*eagerly*) And?
MAURICE. And I was sick.
MICHEL. Ah!
MAURICE. I took too many.
MICHEL. Yes. You've got to know the secret number, dear, otherwise it doesn't work. I wouldn't recommend it as a very sure-fire method myself.
MAURICE. No.
MICHEL. Well, anyway, that's beside the point. Why did you do it? Was it over a lover?
MAURICE. No. It was—something that happened at work.

MICHEL. What happened at work?
MAURICE (*shaking his head*) Nothing.
MICHEL. But I mean, something must have happened...
MAURICE. Nothing happened at work. I'd rather not...
MICHEL. All right, dear—let's forget about it. (*Friendly; holding out his glass*) What about another little drink?

(MAURICE *picks up the brandy bottle and pours a little into the glass*)

(*Tipping the bottle*) Don't worry about Edward's brandy, dear— he can afford it. Aren't you going to join me?
MAURICE (*replacing the bottle on the stool*) I think I'll finish my milk. (*He picks up his glass and moves away* LC)
MICHEL. Cheers! (*He drinks*) I come from a family of suicides, you know. My mother did it when she found her lover in bed with another woman. She took the next plane to Paris and jumped off the Eiffel Tower. (*He pauses*) My father found *his* lover in bed with another man and cut his throat with a safety razor one morning before breakfast. (*He moves to the sofa and sits*) So you see, I know all about it.
MAURICE (*sympathetically*) Yes. (*He sits in the armchair* LC)
MICHEL. The trouble is I haven't inherited their strength of character. I'd be a teeny bit afraid to jump into the unknown just like that. After all, it might be worse than here. (*He pauses*) No. I should only like to kill myself if I could creep back afterwards and see the faces—everybody crying over my body—big splash in the papers. (*He thinks about it for a moment*) But what if they weren't crying? There's a saying about it, isn't there—'you never know your friends until you're dead—and then it's too late'. (*He pauses*) Anyway, I'm not going to do it. Actually, I feel rather better now. I just got a bit depressed in that garden—that's all it was. (*He smiles at Maurice*)

(MAURICE *smiles, but rather shyly*)

MAURICE. I do hope you'll be able to find another job, Michel.
MICHEL. Oh yes, I suppose I will. You know, I think it was terribly mean of Edward to throw me out the way he did. Don't you think it was terribly mean?
MAURICE. I think he was upset about the music.
MICHEL. It's hardly a good enough reason to dismiss anybody for, anyway. He didn't even give me a chance to explain. I mean, you were there.
MAURICE. Yes.
MICHEL. Edward's mad, you know, quite mad.
MAURICE. I don't think... (*He breaks off*)
MICHEL (*looking enquiringly at Maurice*) Yes?
MAURICE. I don't think one person should say another person is mad, without first measuring their own sanity.

MICHEL. If you could tell me how to do that, dear, I'd be delighted to try. Anyway, allow me to know a little more about Edward than you do. After all, you've been here five minutes—I really don't think you're any judge. I could tell you stories. For instance—one day he turned to me and he said, 'Michel, I feel terribly bored this afternoon, let's go out and play with bows and arrows.' I couldn't believe my ears, nor my eyes, when Holmes came up from the cellar with them. (*He pauses*) Well—we went out and started this game. I mean—I wouldn't have minded if we'd shot at birds or something, but he wouldn't allow that. Well—after several hours of hide and seek and shooting those arrows about, I said to him, 'Edward, don't you think you're a bit old for Robin Hood?' Well—he looked at me in a very sinister fashion and then told me to return to the house. I'd only gone a few yards when an arrow whizzed past my head—so close, my dear, that the air fanned my face—and then another, and another, a positive hail of arrows, so I started to run and he pursued me like that all the way back. Later on I told him exactly what I thought about the whole thing and suddenly he started to cry. Oh, he's definitely mad.

(MAURICE, *at this point, does not seem to go on listening. He rises, goes to the fireplace and gazes into the fire*)

But, you know, sometimes he was marvellous. He used to go to the ballet and the opera—we always had a box. We used to have wonderful dinners with champagne. Sometimes we'd fly over to Paris for a few days and he'd buy me all kinds of presents. Oh, he can be charming, but it's the charm of the insane, if you know what I mean. (*He pauses and looks at his watch*) My goodness, it's nearly four a.m. He'll be down for the cards. (*He rises, moves to Maurice and touches him*) Maurice.

(MAURICE *turns*)

Dear Maurice, would you just run up quickly and get my transistor—you could get one of my suits, too, at the same time.

(MAURICE *does not answer*)

(*Insistently*) Maurice.

MAURICE. Look, why don't you ask Mr Kimberley to give it to you.

MICHEL. I already have. You saw how he was. He's just painted it and given it to you. He'll get you another one.

MAURICE. I can't do a thing like that.

MICHEL. Why not?

MAURICE. I—I work here.

MICHEL. Very well. (*He flounces to the tray*) Take my transistor—take my job. (*He pours himself another brandy*)

MAURICE. Stop it! (*The words seem to stick in his throat*) And stop —stop drinking that brandy.

MICHEL. Very well. (*He puts down the glass, moves* RC *and slowly pours the contents of the brandy bottle on to the floor*)

(MAURICE *starts forward and then stops, stricken by the sight*)

(*He lets the last drop out*) Explain that in the morning.

MICHEL *puts the bottle on the table* RC *and exits quickly by the french windows.* MAURICE *looks down at the floor, numbed with shock.*

HOLMES *enters quietly from the hall, with a tea-cloth, and switches on the chandeliers. As if he knew exactly what had happened, he crosses to* RC *and mops up the brandy on the carpet with the tea-cloth.* MAURICE *watches in silence, not knowing or daring to speak to the old man.* HOLMES *takes two packs of cards from the table down* R *and puts them on the table* RC, *then moves the chairs from down* R *and up* R *to* R *and* L *of the table* RC. *He collects the dirty brandy glasses, brandy bottle, and milk glasses, puts them on the tray and picks it up.*

HOLMES *exits quietly to the hall.* MAURICE *goes to the table* RC, *sits* R *of it and fiddles nervously with one of the packs of cards.*

EDWARD *enters from the hall and stands quietly in the doorway for a second. He is in his dressing-gown.* MAURICE *sees Edward and rises.* EDWARD *crosses to* L *of the table* RC, *looks at Maurice for a second, and we feel that he, like Holmes, knew exactly what had happened. He smiles and motions to Maurice to sit, and seats himself* L *of the table.* MAURICE *resumes his seat.* EDWARD *motions him to commence the game.* MAURICE *shuffles the cards and deals as—*

the CURTAIN *falls*

ACT II

SCENE I

SCENE—*The same. Morning, some weeks later.*

When the CURTAIN *rises,* MAURICE *and* EDWARD *enter by the french windows.* MAURICE *wears a Red Indian brave's head-band with feathers.* EDWARD *wears a Red Indian Chief's head-dress. Both carry bows and quivers with arrows.* EDWARD *gives his bow and quiver to* MAURICE *who puts them with his own on the table* R. *Neither of them removes the feather bands.* EDWARD *flexes his hands, looks at his fingers and holds them in front of him.*

MAURICE. How are they?

EDWARD (*crossing to* LC) So-so. (*He sits on the sofa*) I feel rather puffed. (*He picks up a copy of 'The Times' from the stool and leans back*) Pity about the arrow.

MAURICE (*crossing to* LC) Yes.

EDWARD. Anyway, it was a good game. (*He reads*)

MAURICE (*enthusiastically*) Yes—it was. (*He sits in the armchair* LC)

EDWARD (*musing*) What shall we drink? What would you say to Campari—clean and refreshing?

MAURICE. Yes, that would be nice.

EDWARD. Ring for Holmes. (*He reads*)

(MAURICE *rises, moves to the fireplace and rings the bell*)

Oh. Henry Rollo's dead. Did I ever tell you about Henry Rollo?

MAURICE. No, you didn't.

EDWARD. How was your lesson this morning?

MAURICE (*sitting in the armchair* LC) He seemed to think I was making progress.

EDWARD. It sounded as if you were, what I heard. I think you're learning remarkably quickly.

MAURICE. It's very kind of you to let me have lessons. I would like to say—thank you.

EDWARD. Not at all. Your progress is my thanks. (*He pauses*) Oh, who do you think I met in town yesterday?

MAURICE. I don't know.

EDWARD. Michel.

(*Some nervousness seems to creep over* MAURICE)

Yes, he . . .

(HOLMES *enters from the hall*)

Ah, Holmes. Campari—soda, please.

HOLMES. Very good, sir.

(HOLMES *exits to the hall*)

EDWARD (*after a pause*) What was I saying? (*He pauses briefly*) Oh, yes,—Michel. I was going to hurry by, but he stopped me and asked me to take a coffee with him. He was rather charming—full of apologies and regret for the way he'd behaved when he worked for me—said he'd give anything to come back. Apparently, the night he left me he made some silly attempt at suicide. He said it was over me. It seemed all his tantrums and bad behaviour had been because he thought I didn't like him. I ended up feeling rather mean for dismissing him the way I did—so I asked him for tea this afternoon. He seems terribly lonely and I feel that perhaps I was a little unjust. (*He pauses*)

(MAURICE *is silent*)

You don't mind, I hope, Maurice?
MAURICE (*pulling himself together*) No—no, of course not.

(EDWARD *takes a small pin-up cutting from his pocket*)

EDWARD. Holmes found this on the carpet this morning. I just wanted to ask if it was yours? (*He holds the cutting at arm's length*) Quite a charming pose, really—if you like that sort of thing.
MAURICE (*crimson*) Oh. (*He puts out his hand for the cutting*) Yes—it is mine. It must have fallen . . .
EDWARD. A friend?
MAURICE. Oh, no. I've never—met . . . (*His voice trails off*)
EDWARD. A pin-up, perhaps?
MAURICE. Yes—well—I cut it out of a newspaper.
EDWARD. *Daily Mirror*, no doubt. (*He hands the cutting to Maurice*) Better put it away.
MAURICE. It must have fallen out of my wallet. (*He takes an old shabby wallet from his pocket and hastily puts the cutting in it*)
EDWARD. 'Note case', Maurice—you must remember to say 'note case'. (*He leans over, hand outstretched*) May I see it?

(MAURICE *hands the wallet to Edward*)

Of course, I can understand you calling it a wallet. (*He turns it over*) Very shabby, isn't it? We shall have to see about getting you another—black crocodile, perhaps—would you like that?
MAURICE (*shifting uncomfortably*) It's all right, really.
EDWARD. Oh, but it isn't all right—it's very shabby. I suggest we throw it away—take the things out, of course—but you'd better do that. (*He returns the wallet to Maurice*)

(MAURICE *sits holding the wallet. He does not want to open it*)

Let's throw it away now, shall we? Then we can go shopping. (*He smiles as if to a child*) I should enjoy taking you shopping, Maurice.

(MAURICE, *very embarrassed, takes everything out of the wallet, and with his knees together, makes an untidy little pile on his lap. A pound note, some creased papers, an N.H.S. card, the pin-up and then, one at a time, some small photographs*)

(*He watches in silence until Maurice gets to the photographs, and then speaks*) Maurice, I've never asked you—what do you think about women? I presume from that little cut-out you do think about women.

MAURICE (*crimson*) I—yes—I do—sometimes.

EDWARD. What do you think?

MAURICE (*hesitantly*) I don't know.

EDWARD. Now, now! You must know what you think.

MAURICE. I suppose—I just sort of wonder about them. I've never known any, you see—very well. (*The wallet is now empty*) Where shall I . . .? (*He does not know where to put the wallet*)

EDWARD (*rising and taking the wallet from Maurice*) Into the fire with it. (*He moves to the fireplace and nonchalantly tosses the wallet into the fire*) It's had its day. (*He moves to Maurice*)

(MAURICE *bundles the things on his knee together*)

MAURICE. I'll take these upstairs.

EDWARD (*standing behind Maurice*) Don't bother now, there's no hurry. (*He leans over Maurice's shoulder*) Are those photographs?

MAURICE. Yes

EDWARD. How delightful.

(MAURICE *clutches them tighter*)

Aren't you going to show me?

MAURICE (*after a slight pause*) They—they aren't very . . . I don't think you'd . . .

EDWARD. But I would—I'd be most interested, Maurice. (*He leans over more*) Family, are they?

MAURICE. No.

EDWARD. Pets?

MAURICE. No. (*He twiddles the corners*)

EDWARD. Could they perhaps be of girls, Maurice? (*He pauses*) Do show me.

(MAURICE *suddenly turns the photographs over and hands them one at a time to Edward, speaking rather quickly*)

MAURICE. That one—that was a girl in the house next to us. She let me take it over the wall, once.

EDWARD. Sun-bathing?

MAURICE. Yes.

EDWARD. I love the sun, don't you? One day, perhaps, we'll have a little holiday in the sun—the real sun, Maurice—not the insipid apology we get here. And that one?

MAURICE (*handing the next photograph to Edward*) That's a girl that used to come into Austin Reed's—I took it outside the shop.
EDWARD. Austin Reed's have a woman's department, have they?
MAURICE. No. She used to come in and buy things for her boy-friend—ties and socks and things. I just asked her one day if I could take a snap of her. She said she didn't mind. I took it outside on the pavement.
EDWARD. That's Aquascutum opposite, isn't it—or is it Jaeger? Well, never mind. (*He points to the next photograph*) What's that one?
MAURICE. It's the girl in the grocer's. The shop on the corner of our street—she works there.
EDWARD. Lovely face—most interesting.
MAURICE. Yes. (*Keenly*) Yes—she . . .
EDWARD. What breed?

(MAURICE *looks blankly at Edward*)

That delightful pussy-cat on the counter. What is it?
MAURICE (*after a slight pause*) It's the shop-cat—tabby.
EDWARD. Oh. Yes—well, never mind. I used to have a dear cat, once. A Siamese—very beautiful—perhaps you've noticed the little grave in the garden?
MAURICE. No—I . . .
EDWARD. I'll point it out to you. (*He leans over*) Have you got a special photograph, Maurice? Particularly special?

(MAURICE *hesitates, then turns over the last photograph*)

MAURICE. There's this one.
EDWARD. May I? (*He takes the photograph and there is a pause as he studies it*) Ah. Very touching—little semi-detached in the background. She looks a very nice girl. Tell me about her, Maurice.
MAURICE (*after a slight pause*) She was in my class at school.
EDWARD. Ah—school friends. I missed all that, you know—having a tutor. I suppose you've known her a long time, then.
MAURICE. Yes—well, quite a long time.
EDWARD. Met her often, of course.
MAURICE. When she could—she couldn't always.
EDWARD. Oh?
MAURICE. No—sometimes she didn't . . . (*His voice trails off*)
EDWARD (*kindly*) Didn't what, Maurice?
MAURICE. Didn't want to—she didn't always want to go out.
EDWARD. Oh, well, one doesn't always, does one? And what did you do when you did go out?
MAURICE. Pictures.
EDWARD. *Only* pictures?
MAURICE. I used to ask her if she'd like to do something else, but she wouldn't. She was keen on the pictures.

EDWARD. And after the pictures—little dinners?
MAURICE. No—she never wanted to go to a café. We just walked back—we lived quite near each other, you see. I walked her to her house and then I went home.
EDWARD (*after a pause*) Did you kiss her, Maurice?
MAURICE (*after a long pause; in a whisper*) No.
EDWARD (*brightly*) No, of course not. It must have been all very idyllic, I suppose—these young friendships founded at school. And where is she now?
MAURICE. I don't see her now. I don't know where she is.
EDWARD. Oh, but that's a pity, isn't it? But then, of course, we all change, don't we? The sort of people we liked yesterday, we don't like today. Except for the very special people. But wasn't she one of those very special people, Maurice?
MAURICE. She didn't want to see me any more. And my father said I shouldn't be in late if I had a job to do. (*He looks very unhappy*) But anyway, she didn't want to see me.
EDWARD. Young women are very unkind. All women are very unkind. You know, Maurice—after my mother went away—I wouldn't go near a woman. Sometimes vague aunts and distant cousins of my father used to visit the house. When they came, I used to run away and hide. My father used to threaten me, but I would never come out until they'd gone. (*He pauses*) Now—well— I realize women exist somewhere—(*he gestures*) outside—but they might as well be on another planet as far as I'm concerned. (*He pauses*) But you, Maurice, are a young man. You are bound to have a little curiosity. All that I ask, is that you retain that curiosity for such time as you may spend away from this house.
MAURICE. Yes—yes, I will. Anyway—I don't think I . . .
EDWARD. Let me give you a piece of advice. Women—Maurice—are like cats. They appear to be with you, but they walk by themselves. (*He looks thoughtfully at the photographs*) Now, what about these? I think—the best thing . . . . (*He suddenly throws the photographs into the fire*)

(MAURICE *starts up and stares at the burning photographs*)

Dead people, Maurice—dead people. (*He moves to the alcove, where there is a stand with a partly done jig-saw puzzle on it. He picks up a box of jig-saw pieces from the chair* R *and from time to time during the following, he adds pieces to the puzzle*)

(HOLMES *enters from the hall, carrying a tray with a bottle of Campari, two glasses, a soda syphon and ice. He crosses and puts the tray on the table* RC)

Oh, Holmes, do you remember Henry Rollo?
HOLMES. Indeed I do, sir.
EDWARD. He died yesterday.
HOLMES. I am very sorry to hear it, sir.

EDWARD. We grew up together, Henry Rollo and I.

(HOLMES *collects the bows, quivers and arrows*)

He lived next door for fifteen years and I was never allowed to play with him. They would never tell me why—something funny in the family, they said—I found out what it was eventually. (*He takes the feather band off his head and hands it to Holmes as if it were a hat*) Didn't I, Holmes?

HOLMES. Yes, sir.

(MAURICE *removes his head-band and* HOLMES *takes it with slightly less deference*)

EDWARD. I wonder what happened to Professor Dornhorst, eh, Holmes?

HOLMES. Perhaps he died, sir.

EDWARD (*smiling*) Yes, yes, perhaps he did. I am not by nature a malicious man, but I would like to think it was an unpleasant death.

(HOLMES *allows himself the very faintest glimmer of a smile*)

HOLMES. Yes, sir. (*He pauses briefly*) Will that be all, sir?

EDWARD. Yes, thank you, Holmes.

(HOLMES *exits to the hall.* MAURICE *goes to the table* RC *and mixes the drinks*).

Professor Dornhorst was my tutor. I can see him now—the cold blue eyes and the thick bull neck. He was a very 'Spartan' man—very keen on ice-cold baths and naked whippings over the backs of stools. The kind of man who would have been excellent at supervising the 'showers' in Nazi concentration camps. (*Musing*) Perhaps he did. (*He concentrates on the puzzle*)

(MAURICE *picks up a drink, moves to Edward and hands it to him*)

(*He hands the box of jig-saw pieces to Maurice*) But I was telling you about Henry Rollo. For years he and I conducted a kind of communication in sign language, from my bedroom window to his garden. Then, one day, when I was twelve and he was fifteen, he climbed the drain-pipe up to my room. He used to climb up once or twice a week in the middle of the night and stay until it began to get light. (*He crosses and sits in the armchair* LC) One day Professor Dornhorst caught us—there was a big fuss with my father and I was subjected to one of those 'punishments'. Professor Dornhorst was very keen on 'punishments'. You were lucky, Maurice, to get your hidings from your father. (*He pauses*)

(*They look at each other then* MAURICE *adds some pieces to the jig-saw*)

Shortly afterwards the Rollo family moved away. I used to read about Henry, though—through the years. He became a brilliant lawyer. When my father died I wrote him a letter—don't really know what induced me. He never replied. (*He pauses*)

(MAURICE *puts the jig-saw pieces on the chair* R *and collects his drink*)

Only three years older than me. I wonder what sort of stories people will tell about me when I die? I suppose there'll be a few bits and pieces in the papers. *Times* obituary column'll be very respectable, of course. 'Mr Edward Kimberley died yesterday at his home in Highgate. He was the only son of the late Sir Oswald Kimberley. Mr Kimberley was unmarried.' The others might be rather different. 'Wealthy Eccentric found dead in bed.' It is my intention, you see, to die in bed. 'Starting next week—a succession of articles by young men who have acted as paid companions to the deceased.' Beginning with—'My life with Edward Kimberley—Intimate revelations by Michael Sanderson.' Maurice, I hope *you* wouldn't stoop to that?

MAURICE. No (*He crosses to* LC) I would never do that—never.

EDWARD. They would pay a lot of money for these stories, you know, particularly if you colour them up a bit. It's very tempting if you haven't any money.

MAURICE (*hovering*) If I hadn't a penny in the world, I wouldn't do that. Please believe me.

EDWARD. I do. (*He hands his glass to Maurice to refill*) Michel would certainly cash in on it.

(MAURICE *puts his glass on the stool, crosses to the table* RC *and refills Edward's glass*)

I suppose part of Michel's charm is his utter lack of moral sense—and his flagrant dishonesty, of course.

(MAURICE *crosses and hands the drink to Edward*)

Your charm, Maurice, is of another sort. In fact, you are the antithesis of Michel. You are completely trustworthy, completely honest, *terribly* loyal—and just a teeny weeny bit dull.

(MAURICE *stands stock still and stares at Edward. He is unspeakably hurt. After some moments he turns and goes to the hall door.* EDWARD *waits until Maurice has nearly reached the door before speaking*)

Maurice Morris, where are you going?

MAURICE (*stopping*) Nowhere.

EDWARD. Well, that doesn't sound very interesting. Why don't you stay here with me?

MAURICE (*turning; after a slight hesitation*) Very well. (*He crosses, sits obediently on the sofa and stares straight in front of him*)

(*There is a pause*)

EDWARD. Maurice, I've just been rather insulting—you may retaliate if you wish. (*He pauses*) Go on. Consider yourself free to say anything you like.
MAURICE. I—(*he looks at Edward*) can't.
EDWARD. Why not?

(MAURICE *sort of crumples, puts his head on his hands and weeps*)

(*He rises, moves to Maurice and puts a hand on his shoulder*) You must forgive me. I didn't mean to upset you.

(MAURICE *looks up at Edward, tears running down his cheeks*)

MAURICE (*like a child*) I just haven't anything to say, that's all. I can't think of anything to say.

(EDWARD *takes a silk handkerchief from his pocket and gently dabs Maurice's eyes as a man might to a small boy, then he gives Maurice a cigarette and lights it for him*)

EDWARD. Maurice—I am deeply sorry.

(MAURICE *has stopped crying and draws deeply on his cigarette*)

MAURICE. No. You see, it's right what you say. I am dull—I'm very dull. I can never think of anything to say. I don't know how to be witty and smart like Michel.
EDWARD. You must get that idea out of your head. Michel may have had moments of fleeting wit—but I can assure you, underneath he is a sad and sorry creature. I would have no wish to be like Michel if I were you.
MAURICE. Oh, but, Edward . . .
EDWARD. 'Edward'? (*He smiles*) You called me 'Edward'. Our friendship is progressing. What were you going to say?
MAURICE (*looking more relaxed*) You see, Edward, I don't want to be like Michel. I want to be like you.
EDWARD. Really (*He is pleased*) Like me? But, my dear Maurice, let me assure you, underneath my veneer I, too, am a sad and sorry creature. (*He laughs*) We are all sad and sorry creatures under the skin.

(EDWARD *and* MAURICE *smile at each other*)

Let me get you another drink. (*He collects his own and Maurice's glasses, refills them, returns Maurice's glass to him then sits in the armchair* LC *and looks kindly over at Maurice*) Maurice, were you unhappy as a little boy?
MAURICE (*slowly*) I don't know.
EDWARD. What do you mean—you don't know?
MAURICE. Well, it's funny—but I can't seem to remember.
EDWARD. You don't remember being a little boy?
MAURICE. No. Not really.

C

EDWARD (*after a pause*) Tell me about your father. You've never told me much about him.
MAURICE. He was a salesman.
EDWARD. Yes, you told me that.
MAURICE. He worked very hard.
EDWARD. Yes, I'm sure he did. But tell me about the relationship between you. Were you happy together? Did he play games with you when you were small?

(MAURICE *shakes his head*)

Did he read to you?
MAURICE. He didn't like books.
EDWARD. Well, what did you do together?
MAURICE. I had lessons.
EDWARD. I wasn't talking about school. I was asking you what you did in the evenings and the weekends.
MAURICE. My father gave me lessons.
EDWARD. Lessons in what?
MAURICE. Lessons in selling.

(EDWARD *looks puzzled*)

He taught me how to sell.
EDWARD (*rising*) How did he do that? (*He sits* L *of Maurice on the sofa*)
MAURICE. He had a wooden counter and a stack of shelves. He made them himself. He had lots of shirts and ties—seconds they were—I think he used to borrow them from the shop where he worked, but I'm not sure—they were all in bags. And he had a till and a mirror—and a swivler.
EDWARD. Swivler?
MAURICE. For the ties. (*He gestures*)
EDWARD. What did you do?
MAURICE. I used to stand behind the counter with my best suit on and my best collar and tie—and I used to serve him—with the shirts and things.
EDWARD. Your father?
MAURICE. Yes. He used to pretend to be different customers, you see.
EDWARD. And you were the salesman?
MAURICE. Yes.

(EDWARD *looks at Maurice with pity*)

EDWARD. How old were you then?
MAURICE. I think I was about eight in the beginning. He worked so hard on me, my father, and I was such a disappointment to him. I wasn't ever a good salesman.
EDWARD (*smiling*) I can well believe it. It was a totally wrong profession for you. Your father should have taught you something else.

MAURICE (*reasonably*) He didn't know anything else.

(EDWARD *studies the tips of his fingers for a moment and then looks up at Maurice*)

EDWARD. Tell me, Maurice, did your father hit you very often?
MAURICE. Not often.
EDWARD. Did you hate him?
MAURICE. My father?
EDWARD. Your father—did you hate him?
MAURICE (*after a slight pause; sadly*) No—I loved him.
EDWARD. I suppose I loved my father, too. I only thought I hated him. (*He rises, goes to the desk, takes a small packet from the drawer and returns to* L *of Maurice*) Maurice, I have something for you—(*he holds out the packet*) a little present.
MAURICE. For me? (*His eyes light up and he rises*)
EDWARD. Yes—take it.

(MAURICE *takes the packet and looks like a small boy*)

Open it.

(MAURICE *slowly unwraps the paper until he comes to a small box. He lifts the lid*)

I hope you like it.
MAURICE. It's beautiful. (*He takes from the box a small gold cigarette lighter, a replica of Edward's*) I can't believe it's for me. It's just like yours.
EDWARD. It's got your initial on it.

(MAURICE *looks at Edward and smiles.*
HOLMES *enters from the hall*)

HOLMES. Lunch is served, sir.
EDWARD. Thank you, Holmes.

(HOLMES *crosses and collects the drinks tray and glasses.* MAURICE *admires the lighter and tries it out*)

(*To Holmes*) What has Atherton arranged for us today, Holmes?
HOLMES (*slightly straightening his bent back*) 'Lobster Thermidor', sir.
EDWARD. Splendid! (*He whispers to Maurice*) It's lobster. Shall we go in?

EDWARD *puts an arm around* MAURICE'S *shoulder. They move towards the hall door.* MAURICE, *like a small boy, flicks the lighter on and off as—*

the LIGHTS BLACK-OUT

Scene 2

When the LIGHTS *come up, the daylight is beginning to fade and the french windows are closed.* MICHEL *is sitting on the sofa. He fills a cigarette packet with cigarettes from the box on the stool.*

MICHEL. Maurice, Maurice, I call that very sly of you.

(MAURICE *enters from the hall. He is wearing a new and very elegant suit*)

(*He rises. Over-effusive*) Hello. (*He gives Maurice a limp handshake*) How are you?

MAURICE (*stiffly*) I'm—I'm very well, thank you.

MICHEL (*eyeing him up and down*) You look it, I must say. (*He fingers the lapels of Maurice's jacket*) Turn round slowly.

(MAURICE *hesitates then slowly turns*)

Absolute perfection, if you like that sort of thing. You look like a model for Aquascutum, dear.

MAURICE (*pleased*) Thank you.

MICHEL (*sighing*) I'm still in the same rags, as you see. Where's Edward?

MAURICE. He won't be long. Please sit down.

MICHEL (*with mock politeness*) Thank you. (*He sits in the armchair* LC *and crosses his legs*)

(MAURICE *takes out a packet of cigarettes and proffers it to Michel*)

MAURICE. Would you like a cigarette?

MICHEL. Thank you. (*He takes a cigarette*)

(MAURICE *lights Michel's cigarette with his new gold lighter.* MICHEL *looks at him over the top and as* MAURICE *moves away,* MICHEL *catches his wrist*)

(*He takes the lighter*) May I see? (*He looks at the lighter*) Pretty—very pretty. (*He turns it over*) Got the initial 'M' engraved on it, too.

MAURICE. Yes.

MICHEL. My name begins with 'M'. Funny, isn't it? (*He does not give the lighter back to Maurice, but retains it in his hand*)

(*There is a pause.* MAURICE *does not know what to do about the lighter*)

He's still got that terrible garden. I thought perhaps you'd persuade him to do something about it.

MAURICE. I think it's a beautiful garden. I like it.

MICHEL. Oh, yes. I remember. You told me. (*He lifts the lid of the silver box on the table* LC *and drops it down quickly*) He's still got that obscenity, I see.

MAURICE. He was very fond of that dog.
MICHEL (*rising*) Has Edward acquired another car? I saw a little Renault in the drive with the Bentley.
MAURICE. It's mine.
MICHEL. Really? Temporary loan, I suppose. Well, remember the old saying—(*He sings to the tune of 'Coming Round the Mountain'*) 'Oh, you can't take it with you when you go—Oh, you can't take it with you when you go.' (*He mimes conducting*) 'Oh, you can't take it with you.' (*He gives a little skip*) 'Oh, you can't take it with you when you go.'
MAURICE (*calmly*) It's in my name.

(MICHEL *stares at Maurice, speechless and livid.*
EDWARD *enters from the hall.* MICHEL *slips the lighter into his pocket. This is observed by* EDWARD *but he gives no sign of it*)

EDWARD. Michel. (*He crosses to Michel*) I'm so glad you could come. (*He shakes hands with Michel*)

(MAURICE *turns away to the fireplace*)

MICHEL. It's lovely to be here. I've often thought about this room—and you, Edward. I can't tell you how I regret—(*he glances towards Maurice and whispers*) everything.
EDWARD. Sit down, Michel. Maurice will ring for tea. (*He sits in the armchair* LC)

(MICHEL *sits on the sofa.* MAURICE *rings the bell at the fireplace*)

MICHEL. The garden's looking marvellous.
EDWARD. Yes. I'm a bit worried about the tree. If it falls down it'll come straight in here. But you know how I feel about it, Michel, it's been here since I was a little boy. I'd be very unhappy to have it removed. Sit down, Maurice.

(MAURICE *crosses and sits on the chair down* L)

(*To Michel*) Now, tell me, have you found another position?
MICHEL. No, nothing at all. (*He brushes a hand through his hair*) I—haven't been well lately.
EDWARD. I'm sorry.
MICHEL. Oh, it doesn't matter. Everything that happens to me is my own silly fault. I'm very mixed up, you know. I always make such a mess of my life.
EDWARD. I'll have to see what I can do to help.
MICHEL. No, Edward. I don't want you to do anything. You were terribly kind to me and I spoilt everything. Not like Maurice, there—I'm sure Maurice never does anything wrong.

(MAURICE *colours and fingers his collar*)

EDWARD. Give him time. He hasn't been here very long. Oh, I must tell you, Michel. Maurice is blossoming into an excellent pianist.

MICHEL. Really? I didn't think you could play, Maurice.

(MAURICE *colours*.

HOLMES *enters from the hall carrying a tray of tea and a plate of cakes*)

EDWARD. He's having lessons—every morning.

(HOLMES *puts the tray on the table* RC *and the cakes on the stool, then switches on the chandeliers*)

MICHEL (*sighing*) There you are, you see. No amount of lessons would ever turn *me* into a pianist. Really, it's terribly sad, but it just has to be faced, that I've no talent for anything.

EDWARD. Nonsense, Michel, you underestimate yourself.

(HOLMES *closes the window curtains*)

It's getting dark early.

MICHEL. Mm!

(HOLMES *exits to the hall. There is a pause.* MAURICE *is staring into space*)

EDWARD (*kindly*) Maurice, shall we have the tea?

MAURICE (*jumping up*) Oh, yes, yes, I'm sorry. (*He crosses to the table* RC *and pours the tea*)

MICHEL (*casually*) I went to your old firm the other day, Maurice. Austin Reed's. I just happened to be passing so I said to myself—'I'll go in'—a lot of milk for me, please.

(MAURICE *goes on pouring*)

I've never been in there before. I thought I could do with another shirt and a new tie. I thought if I mentioned your name to the man behind the counter, Maurice——

(MAURICE *stiffens*)

—he might let me have some things at cost price—two lumps, please—but it was terribly strange, he tried to pretend you'd never worked there—isn't it odd?

(MAURICE *rather nervously hands Michel a cup of tea*)

'Well,' I said—'I know he has. What's the mystery?'

(MAURICE *hands a cup of tea to Edward*)

He said I must be in the wrong shop. Isn't it funny?

EDWARD. Probably a new man.

MICHEL (*mysteriously*) Mm!

(*There is a pause*)

EDWARD. Maurice, aren't you having any tea?

MAURICE. I'm—I'm not very hungry. Would you excuse me, please.

(MAURICE *crosses and exits quickly to the hall*)

MICHEL. What's the matter with him?

EDWARD. Probably just got stomach-ache. We had lobster for lunch.

MICHEL. He's very reserved—Maurice, isn't he? Very reticent about himself.

EDWARD. Not if you take a little time and trouble. Actually, I'm very pleased with the way he's turning out. He has many excellent qualities.

MICHEL. I suppose he doesn't fall asleep over the cards. Like I used to.

EDWARD. Michel, that wasn't what I meant—as you were very well aware. But as a matter of fact—no, he doesn't fall asleep over the cards. He's always remarkably alert—he wins quite often.

MICHEL. Really?

(*There is a pause*)

Edward—I do regret behaving so badly, when you were so kind to me.

EDWARD. Oh, Michel—don't apologize any more. I was much too dull for you. I think you should find someone younger—someone gay and amusing who would give you a good time—with plenty of money, of course.

MICHEL. That isn't what I want. I want to come back to you, Edward. I promise I would be different.

EDWARD. Nonsense, Michel—you'd be exactly the same. Besides, you could hardly expect me to ask Maurice to go, and he's behaved in an exemplary fashion—besides, I like him.

MICHEL (*sadly*) Yes, of course, Edward. I understand.

(*There is a pause.* EDWARD *rises and goes to the desk*)

EDWARD. Michel, I'd like to give you a small gift—just to tide you over until you find a suitable post.

MICHEL. Oh, no—you mustn't.

EDWARD. Nonsense! (*He sits at the desk, fills in a cheque, extracts it from the book, blots it, then rises and crosses to Michel*)

MICHEL (*slowly lifting his head*) I feel so terribly ashamed.

EDWARD. You won't feel so ashamed when you see the size of the cheque—it's quite small. (*He thrusts the cheque under Michel's nose*)

(MICHEL *takes the cheque but does not look at it*)

MICHEL. Oh, Edward, you are beastly to me.

EDWARD. Because I know you.

(*They smile at each other*)

I'm quite fond of you, really. (*He pauses*) Well, I shall go upstairs for my rest. There's no need for you to rush off. I expect

Maurice will be down in a minute. Pour yourself some more tea. (*He takes a cigarette from his case*) Let me know how you get on.

MICHEL (*rising*) Of course, and thank you, Edward.

(*There is a pause.* EDWARD *stands with his unlit cigarette*)

EDWARD. Oh, Michel—do you think you could give me a light?

(MICHEL's *hand goes instinctively to his pocket and stops.* EDWARD *holds his hand out.* MICHEL *slowly gives him Maurice's lighter.*

EDWARD *smiles, goes to the door and exits to the hall.* MICHEL *looks at the amount of the cheque, smiles, puts it in his pocket, sits on the sofa and drinks his tea.*

MAURICE *enters silently by the french windows and stands looking at Michel. After a moment,* MICHEL, *sensing Maurice's presence, turns*)

MICHEL. Oh Maurice—you startled me. What on earth were you doing in the garden?

MAURICE. I was walking.

MICHEL. Weren't you cold?

MAURICE. No (*He crosses to the fireplace*)

MICHEL. Edward's gone to lie down. He asked me if I'd like to stay for dinner. He's such a sweet man. (*He sprawls on the sofa*)

(*There is a pause*)

I haven't made up my mind, yet, whether to stay or not.

MAURICE (*politely*) Michel. Could I have my lighter, please? (*He crosses behind* MICHEL *to the table* RC)

MICHEL (*finishing his tea*) You could if I had it.

MAURICE. What do you mean?

MICHEL. Edward took it. I suddenly realized I'd forgotten to give it back to you, so I put it down on the table and Edward took it. I wonder why? (*He pauses and takes a cake. Through mouthfuls*) Oh, Maurice, I didn't finish telling you about that man at Austin Reed's. I think you went out of the room, didn't you? Anyway, when he said that I must be in the wrong shop because you'd never worked there, I didn't say anything except—'It's funny.' However, after I'd bought an awful lot of ties and shirts, he turned out to be rather nice and we got quite friendly. I'm going to have coffee with him one day. Anyway, he told me a most extraordinary story—about you—quite extraordinary. I couldn't believe my ears. (*He pauses*)

(MAURICE *is silent*)

Do you know what he said?

MAURICE. No.

MICHEL. Well, wait till I tell you. He said—(*he finishes his mouthful of cake*) he said you tried to strangle a customer.

MAURICE. Oh.

MICHEL. I said to him—'Never! I don't believe you. Was it in the papers?' And he said it was all hushed up. He wouldn't go into any details—absolutely refused to say any more about it at all. But, anyway, aren't you worried having people saying things like that about you?
MAURICE. No.
MICHEL. I mean, he said 'strangle'.
MAURICE. Did he?
MICHEL. You mean—they made it up?
MAURICE. Yes.
MICHEL. Why should they do a thing like that? It'd be slander. Of course, I realize it must have been an exaggeration, but something must have happened. Does Edward know about this story?
MAURICE. No.
MICHEL. Well, I think he ought to be told. I mean, suppose he got to hear of it from somebody else? It would be rather alarming. He might think you were a dangerous person to have about the house. I think the best thing would be to pass it off as a joke. I could do it for you if you liked—before dinner. I would say something casual like . . .
MAURICE. No. I don't want Edward to know.
MICHEL. Well, if you don't want him to know, you ought to leave before he finds out. Somebody will tell him. If he discovered you were working for him under false pretences . . .
MAURICE. It's not false pretences.
MICHEL. I wouldn't like to be in your shoes if he finds out. Tell me, did you try to kill somebody?
MAURICE. No.
MICHEL. There's no smoke without fire. Something must have happened. I remember now the first day I met you, we were talking about suicide and you told me you took a lot of aspirins once over something that happened at work.
MAURICE. Nothing happened. A customer came in to buy a tie—and he undid his tie. Look, I'll show you.

(MICHEL *stares at him*)

Undo your tie.
MICHEL. What for?
MAURICE. I want to demonstrate. (*He undoes his own tie*)
MICHEL. Demonstrate what? (*He laughs*) How to strangle a customer—no, thank you. (*He slides to the upstage end of the sofa, away from Maurice*)
MAURICE (*calmly*) Don't be silly. (*He moves behind the sofa, towards Michel*)

(*There is a slight pause*)

MICHEL. All right. (*He undoes his tie*) Let's play salesmen. (*His tie is undone*) Now what?

(MAURICE *takes his own tie right off and folds it over his hand as he would show a new tie*)

MAURICE (*calmly*) The customer undid his tie and I held various ties up to his neck to see how he liked them. (*He holds his own tie up to Michel's neck*) He was looking in the mirror, of course. I showed him lots of ties—all shades—all materials. He didn't like them. (*He pauses*) I showed him more ties—and more and more. He couldn't make up his mind, he asked to see others. I showed him our entire selection—every tie we had in the shop—he was there for hours.

MICHEL. Go on.

MAURICE. Eventually I said—'This is our entire stock, sir—you have seen every tie that we have in the shop.'

MICHEL. Yes?

MAURICE. I said, 'Which one will you decide on, sir?'

MICHEL. What did he say?

MAURICE. He said he wan't going to have any of them. (*He crosses* R *to the mirror and reties his own tie*)

MICHEL (*after a pause*) But that can't be all. (*He draws his knees up, feet on the sofa, and swivels to face* R *towards Maurice*) Then what happened?

MAURICE. Nothing.

MICHEL (*swinging his legs down on the upstage side of the sofa, still facing Maurice*) Nothing?

MAURICE (*turning; quite calmly*) No. (*He goes to Michel and takes the ends of Michel's tie*) I said, 'Please allow me to tie your own tie, sir.' (*He crosses Michel's tie over*) So I folded it over——

(*A slight uneasiness crosses* MICHEL'S *face*)

—and I put it through—(*he puts Michel's tie through*) and I pulled and I pulled——

(MICHEL *struggles and is pulled to his feet,* R *of Maurice*)

—and I pulled and I pulled——

(MICHEL *chokes*)

—and I pulled—(*he throttles Michel*) and he fell down on the floor. (*Still holding the tie he lowers Michel's dead body to the floor behind the sofa, where it lies with the head downstage. He lets go of the tie and after a brief pause steps over Michel's head and moves to the table* RC) But he'd only had a black-out—he was perfectly all right. (*He pours himself a cup of tea, sits on the sofa and talks to Michel as if he were still alive*) They made such a fuss in the shop. They all came running. I said, 'He's perfectly all right', and he was when they took his tie off. He didn't say anything for a bit—and then he said he wanted the police. (*He drinks some tea*) Anyway, they didn't let him call the police. They took him into the Manager's office and I didn't see him again. (*He takes a cake and eats it*) Anyway, they gave me the sack—just for that—just because I'd tied his tie a bit tight. (*He pauses and eats*) They were beautiful ties, what I showed him—and he didn't like any of them. (*He takes another cake*) I feel terribly hungry.

(EDWARD, *unseen by Maurice, enters quietly from the hall. He is in his dressing-gown and is holding the lighter. He stands and watches Maurice*)

You know, Michel—I even showed him a leather tie. A leather tie is wonderful, but you must always tie it in the same place.

(EDWARD *suddenly notices Michel. He moves quickly to the fireplace, rings the bell, then goes to Michel and tries frantically to loosen the tie round Michel's neck*)

Hello, Edward. I was just telling Michel about leather ties. I think he's gone to sleep. I wanted to explain to him that one must always remember to tie them in the same place. Did you know that, Edward? Did you know you must always tie a leather tie in the same place? (*He takes another cake*) Do you know, Edward, this is my third cake. I feel so terribly hungry. What are we having for dinner, Edward?

(EDWARD *has released the tie from Michel's neck.*
HOLMES *enters from the hall*)

EDWARD (*urgently*) Holmes!
HOLMES (*moving quicker than usual*) Yes, sir?
EDWARD. Holmes, I think we ought to take Mr Sanderson into the garden for a little.
HOLMES, Yes, sir.

(HOLMES *and* EDWARD *drag Michel towards the french windows*)

MAURICE. You ought to hear what he says about it, Edward, behind your back. (*He calls*) Tell Edward, Michel—what you really think about his garden and that terrible mad creeper, as you call it. I think it's a beautiful garden.

(HOLMES *and* EDWARD *exit by the french windows with the body*)

I think this is a marvellous house—an absolutely marvellous house—and I'm so happy—(*he leans back and is suddenly very tired*) so very happy.

MAURICE'S *eyes close as—*

the CURTAIN *falls*

ACT III
Scene 1

Scene—*The same. Midday, about ten days later.*

When the Curtain *rises,* Edward *is playing with a model railway spread out on a table up* R. Holmes *is giving assistance.*

Edward (*excitedly*) They're going to crash, Holmes.

(*Two trains are racing round the track in opposite directions*)
The points, quick.

(Holmes *adjusts the points and the trains miss each other*)
(*He breathes a sigh of relief*) That was a very close thing.

(*The front door bell rings.* Edward *is too absorbed to notice*)

Holmes. The door bell, sir.
Edward. Was it? Damn! Well, you'd better see who it is.
Holmes. Yes, sir.

(Holmes *exits to the hall, leaving the door open*)

Edward (*calling*) Holmes, I'm not at home.

(*There is a pause.* Edward *continues to play with the trains.*
Holmes *enters from the hall, carrying a card on a salver*)

(*Without looking up*) Who was it?
Holmes. A gentleman, sir. I said you were not at home, but he said he'd wait. (*He crosses to* Edward) His card, sir.

(Edward *takes the card and looks closely at it*)

Edward. Oh. (*He pauses briefly*) Well, you'd better show him in.
Holmes. Very good sir.

(Holmes *exits to the hall.* Edward *stops the trains, goes to the fireplace, puts the card on the mantelpiece and stands with his back to the fire*)

(*Off*) Mr Kimberley is in here, sir.

(Holmes *enters from the hall and stands to one side.*
The Man *enters from the hall. He is aged about twenty-seven and wears a white mackintosh. He has shrewd eyes and one can sense his alertness*)

Edward (*calmly*) Good morning. (*He does not offer to shake hands*)

(Holmes *exits to the hall, closing the door behind him*)

MAN. Good morning. I hope I'm not disturbing you.
EDWARD. Not at all. Please sit down. (*He indicates the sofa*)
MAN. Thank you. (*He sits on the sofa*) No, I won't keep you long.

(EDWARD *takes a cigarette from his case and lights it. He does not offer one to the* MAN)

EDWARD. What can I do for you?
MAN. I don't know that you can do anything, Mr Kimberley, but if you'd be kind enough to answer a few questions . . .
EDWARD (*sitting in the armchair* LC) If it's within my power to do so—certainly.
MAN. I believe you know a Mr Michael Sanderson?
EDWARD. That is correct.
MAN. May I ask how well you know him?
EDWARD. He used to work for me.
MAN. In what capacity?
EDWARD. As a companion.
MAN. Residential?
EDWARD. Naturally.
MAN (*after a pause*) How long did he work for you, Mr Kimberley?
EDWARD. I'm not sure, exactly—around six months, I should say.
MAN. When did he leave?
EDWARD. Oh—let me see—it would be just over a month ago.
MAN. Mr Kimberley, do you know where Mr Sanderson is now?
EDWARD. No. I'm afraid I haven't the slightest idea.
MAN (*after a brief pause*) May I ask why he left your employ?
EDWARD. Certainly. He left because I told him to go.
MAN. Why did you dismiss him, Mr Kimberley?
EDWARD. He wasn't suitable.
MAN (*after a slight pause*) Was your parting amicable?
EDWARD. It wasn't unamicable.
MAN. I see. In other words, Mr Sanderson was not upset by his dismissal?
EDWARD. I don't know. I didn't ask him.
MAN. How much notice was he given?
EDWARD. No notice. I just told him to go and he went.

(*There is a pause. The* MAN *takes out a notebook and pencil*)

MAN. Could you tell me the actual date of dismissal?
EDWARD. I don't think I can, off-hand. (*He thinks*) It was a Thursday—it must have been a month ago last Thursday.
MAN (*consulting his notebook*) That would be on the fifteenth of last month?
EDWARD. If you say so.
MAN. But you remember it was a Thursday?

EDWARD. Yes.

MAN (*after a slight pause*) Mr Kimberley, was the day of his dismissal the last time you saw Mr Sanderson?

EDWARD. No. I saw him just over a week ago.

MAN. May I ask where that was?

EDWARD. I bumped into him in town. We had coffee together. The day following he came here for tea.

MAN. What day was that?

EDWARD. I think it was a week last Friday.

MAN. I would be grateful if you would tell me the exact day, Mr Kimberley.

(EDWARD *rises, goes to the fireplace and rings the bell*)

EDWARD. My manservant will be able to tell you, he has an excellent memory. (*He rests his hand on the mantelshelf*) May I ask *you* a question?

MAN. Yes, sir.

EDWARD. Why do you want to know?

MAN. Mr Sanderson has been missing from his lodgings for ten days. We have been asked to try and trace his whereabouts.

EDWARD. Perhaps he's gone on holiday?

MAN. Without his luggage? I don't think so, Mr Kimberley.

EDWARD. Stranger things have happened.

(*The* MAN *gives a half-smile.*
HOLMES *enters from the hall*)

Holmes, would you come here for a moment, please.

HOLMES. Yes, sir. (*He moves to* L *of Edward*)

EDWARD. Holmes, this gentleman is anxious to discover what day it was that Mr Sanderson came here for tea. Are you able to tell him?

HOLMES. Yes, sir. (*He does not look at the Man*) It was a week last Friday, sir.

EDWARD. Thank you, Holmes, you may go. (*To the Man*) A week last Friday.

(HOLMES *moves to the hall door*)

MAN (*rising*) Just a minute, please.

(HOLMES *does not stop*)

EDWARD (*smiling at the Man*) He's rather deaf. (*To Holmes, without raising his voice*) Holmes, just one moment.

HOLMES (*stopping and turning*) Yes, sir?

EDWARD. Holmes, this gentleman has a further question for you. Perhaps you'd be kind enough to try and help him. (*He gestures to the Man*)

MAN. Mr Holmes. Have you any particular reason for remembering that it was a week last Friday that Mr Sanderson came here for tea?

HOLMES (*stiffly*) We don't have many visitors here, sir.
MAN. You are quite sure you have not mistaken the day?
HOLMES. No, sir. It was the day the cook prepared lobster for lunch and that same morning made a great many cakes for tea.
EDWARD. You're absolutely right, Holmes. It was the day we had lobster for lunch. Thank you, Holmes. (*To the Man*) Can he go now?
MAN. Yes.
EDWARD. Thank you, Holmes.

(HOLMES *exits to the hall.* EDWARD *moves to the sideboard and pours a drink for himself*)

Forgive me if I pour myself a drink. If you have many more questions, perhaps you would care to join me?
MAN. I won't, sir, thank you very much.
EDWARD (*tetchily*) Well, do sit down and then I can and it's less like an inquisition.

(*The* MAN *sits on the sofa*)

(*He sits in the armchair* LC) Now, what else would you like to ask me?
MAN. Tell me about your cook, Mr Kimberley.
EDWARD. Atherton? Absolutely splendid—*cordon bleu*, you know.
MAN. Mr or Mrs Atherton?
EDWARD. Funny thing you should ask me that. I don't know—don't think I've ever seen Atherton close to—fleeting glimpses. I think it's a woman—but it could be a man. Ask Holmes, he deals with all the kitchen arrangements. I'm really only interested in the end product, you see. (*He smiles*)
MAN. Is Mr or Mrs Atherton residential?
EDWARD. Oh—non-resident.
MAN. How long in your employ?
EDWARD. Again you'd better ask Holmes. I think about a year. Yes—I think I noticed a slight change in the style of cooking about a year ago. But I've no complaints at all—really. The soufflés would make your mouth water.
MAN. And was this—er—'Atherton' here the afternoon Mr Sanderson came to tea?
EDWARD. Well—there were some delicious fairy cakes, I remember. (*He smiles*) But I believe Atherton only works a half-day—makes the preparations for tea and dinner and leaves after lunch. Holmes sees to the rest.
MAN. How long has Mr Holmes been with you?
EDWARD. Holmes has always been here. He was with my father. His father with my grandfather.
MAN. May I ask about his relationship with Mr Sanderson?
EDWARD (*rising and moving up* RC) Relationship? They had no relationship. (*He studies the train lay-out*)

MAN. What I mean is, Mr Kimberley—did they get on together—or did they ever bandy words?
EDWARD. Bandy words? They never spoke to each other.
MAN. I see. When Mr Sanderson came here for tea, a week last Friday, were you alone together?
EDWARD. No. My new companion was present.
MAN. Could you give me his name, please.
EDWARD. 'Morris.' 'Maurice Morris.'
MAN. Is Mr Morris working for you now?
EDWARD. He is. (*He moves* LC)
MAN (*after a slight pause*) Had they met before—Mr Morris and Mr Sanderson?
EDWARD. Yes. They met the day I dismissed Mr Sanderson and let me hasten to add—before you ask me—they had no relationship.
MAN. Thank you, Mr Kimberley.

(EDWARD *sits in the armchair* LC)

When Mr Sanderson came here for tea, did he say anything to you about his future plans?
EDWARD. He seemed to be under the impression that there was no future.
MAN. He was in a depressed state?
EDWARD. Yes.
MAN (*after a pause*) Would you say, Mr Kimberley, that Mr Sanderson had suicidal tendencies?
EDWARD. No more than any other mixed-up young man.
MAN. There were no good reasons why he should commit suicide?
EDWARD. People never commit suicide for good reasons, only bad.
MAN. Do you know of any bad reason why he should commit suicide?
EDWARD. Well, his parents killed themselves rather dramatically, I believe. Anyway, that's what he said—but then the truth was not Michel's strong point.
MAN. 'Michel'?
EDWARD. That's what I used to call him.
MAN (*after a pause*) Mr Kimberley, to go back to the tea party . . .
EDWARD. No party—just tea.
MAN. Did you get the impression that Mr Sanderson was worried about anything?
EDWARD. Only himself. He worried constantly about himself.
MAN (*after a slight pause*) At what time did he leave your house that afternoon?
EDWARD. Well, I didn't look at my watch at the time, but I think it must have been a little after five o'clock.

MAN. Who saw him to the door?
EDWARD. My manservant, naturally.
MAN. And you have no idea where Mr Sanderson went when he left here?
EDWARD. No idea whatsoever.
MAN (*after a slight pause; rising*) Well, Mr Kimberley—I don't think I need trouble you any further. I wonder if I could just have a few words with Mr Morris?
EDWARD. I don't think he's back, yet—he went shopping for me. However, he should be in any moment now. Would you care to wait? (*He rises*)
MAN. I will, if you don't mind. Would you like me to wait in the hall?
EDWARD. No, no, wait in here—more comfortable. Or perhaps you might care to look at the garden—(*he gestures towards the french windows*) rather wild—but quite interesting. Anyway, I have a few things I want to attend to, so if you'll excuse me . . .? (*He moves to the hall door*) Help yourself to anything you want—(*he gestures*) cigarettes in the boxes. (*He waves*) Good morning.
MAN. Good morning, Mr Kimberley.

(EDWARD *exits to the hall. The* MAN *looks slowly round the room. He wanders to the desk, picks up some letters, glances at them and replaces them. Then he looks at the blotting pad. He extracts the top sheet and puts it quickly into his pocket. He wanders* LC *and his glance falls on the silver box on the table* LC. *He casually lifts the lid, sees the eye in the box and takes a closer look. He takes a clean white handkerchief from his pocket, tips the eye into it and puts it in his pocket. He closes the box, crosses and gazes out of the french windows.*

MAURICE *enters from the hall, laden with parcels. The* MAN *turns*)

MAURICE (*as he enters; excitedly*) Edward . . . (*He sees the man, stops and looks around*) Oh. Excuse me. (*He turns to go*)
MAN (*crossing to* LC) Mr Morris?
MAURICE (*turning*) Yes?
MAN. Could I speak to you for a moment? (*He displays his identity card in its case*)
MAURICE. Oh. Let me put these down. (*He puts the parcels on the sofa. He has changed. His manner is relaxed, almost confident. He looks at the card and then at the Man, betraying nothing. His voice is calm and pleasant*) Oh. Something to do with the car?
MAN. No, Mr Morris. Cars are not my department. Just a few questions.

(*There is a pause as* MAURICE *removes his overcoat and puts it on the sofa*)

MAURICE. Perhaps you'd like to sit down?
MAN. Thank you, no.

(MAURICE *sits on the sofa*)

Mr Morris, I should like to ask you about a Mr Michael Sanderson.
MAURICE. Michael Sanderson? (*He looks puzzled*) Oh—Michel—Edward always called him 'Michel'. Yes?
MAN. I believe you met Mr Sanderson?
MAURICE. Yes, I did.
MAN. Do you think you could tell me when that was?
MAURICE. Well, he used to work here, you see, before me.
MAN. Yes, but when did you first meet him?
MAURICE. The day I came here for an interview.
MAN. Can you tell me what day that was?
MAURICE. Well, I've been here just over a month. It was a Thursday, a month last Thursday.
MAN. And when did you commence employment here, Mr Morris?
MAURICE. The same day. I began that day.
MAN. The day Mr Sanderson left?
MAURICE. Yes.
MAN (*after a pause*) Tell me, Mr Morris—did you have any conversation with Mr Sanderson?
MAURICE. Yes, a little.
MAN. Did you get the impression that he was upset that you had come to take over his job?
MAURICE. No. I don't think he minded very much. He and Mr Kimberley had been getting on each other's nerves.
MAN. I see. (*He pauses*) Have you seen Mr Sanderson since then, Mr Morris?
MAURICE. Yes, he came here for tea after that.
MAN. Were you present?
MAURICE. Yes, we all had tea together.
MAN. What impression did you get of Mr Sanderson?
MAURICE. Well, I didn't get any impression, really. He didn't talk to me much.
MAN. Were you alone with him at all?
MAURICE. No. Mr Kimberley was here all the time.
MAN. And you formed no impression of Mr Sanderson? You didn't notice whether he seemed happy or unhappy?
MAURICE. I remember he said he hadn't been well. Oh, yes—and I remember he said—something about not having any talent.
MAN. Talent for what, Mr Morris?
MAURICE. I don't know—unless it was—we'd been talking about playing the piano, and I can play and he can't—that might have been what he meant.
MAN. I see. (*He pauses*) Did he mention his plans for the future?
MAURICE. No, he didn't say.
MAN. Did you notice anything else about him, Mr Morris?

MAURICE (*thinking*) I remember he was hungry—he ate a lot of cakes. They'd all gone by the time he left.
MAN. When he left, who saw him to the door?
MAURICE. Oh, Holmes—the manservant.
MAN. Well, I don't think there are any further questions, Mr Morris, thank you.
MAURICE (*rising*) Is Michel in some kind of trouble?
MAN. I'm afraid I can't answer that, Mr Morris. I don't know. Mr Sanderson has been missing from his lodgings for the last ten days. (*He moves to the hall door*)
MAURICE. Oh. (*He follows the Man to the door. Brightly*) Perhaps he's gone on holiday.

(*The MAN gives a half-smile*)

MAN. His friends don't seem to think so, Mr Morris. (*He indicates the train set*) Has Mr Kimberley a son?
MAURICE. No. (*Innocently*) He doesn't have any children.
MAN (*looking at Maurice*) Thank you for your help, Mr Morris. Good morning.
MAURICE. Good morning.

The MAN *exits to the hall.* MAURICE *watches him go then takes a gold cigarette case from his pocket. It is a replica of Edward's.* MAURICE *takes a cigarette and lights it with his lighter as—*

the LIGHTS BLACK-OUT

SCENE 2

SCENE—*The same. The evening of the same day.*

When the LIGHTS *come up, the curtains are closed and the lights are on.* EDWARD *is sitting on the sofa.* MAURICE *is standing* L *of the stool. They are nearing the end of a game of Pairs and the cards that are left are lying face downwards spread over the stool.* EDWARD *turns up two cards that do not match. He sighs and turns them back on their faces.* MAURICE, *who is winning, turns up a card and then one of Edward's makes a pair*)

MAURICE. Ah! (*He turns up two more which pair and then with bated breath he turns up and pairs the last four on the table. He looks at Edward in triumph*) Mine! I've won. I've won. Poor Edward.
EDWARD. Yes, Maurice.
MAURICE (*collecting the cards together*) What's the matter?
EDWARD. Nothing.
MAURICE. Are you cross because I won?
EDWARD. Don't be a child.

(*There is a pause.* MAURICE *shuffles the cards*)

MAURICE. Get me a drink, Edward.

(EDWARD *gives Maurice a strange look, rises, moves to the sideboard and pours two brandies*)

(*He sits on the sofa*) Oh, Edward—I meant to ask you—what's happened to the eye? I found it was missing this afternoon.

EDWARD. Can't you guess? Presumably our visitor of this morning took it away in his pocket.

(MAURICE *laughs behind his hand*)

MAURICE. Oh, how terribly funny—a dog's eye.

EDWARD. I don't find it very funny.

MAURICE. Oh, but it is. Can't you imagine them dissecting it—having it analysed . . . (*He pauses. Ingeniously*) Do you suppose they think we killed Michel? Just because he's been missing for ten days. I mean, thousands of people do that—don't they, Edward—walk out and never come back.

(EDWARD *silently hands Maurice his drink*)

I should have told that man I was asleep when Michel left, you know—I just didn't because you told me not to. I suppose you thought it might have made it a bit awkward for you. Of course, I see what you mean.

EDWARD (*quietly*) Maurice—if you prefer to tell the truth about that afternoon—please do so when that man comes back.

MAURICE (*quickly*) Comes back—why should he come back?

EDWARD (*wearily*) Oh, he will, never fear.

MAURICE. I don't fear, Edward—why should I? Anyway, I'd better stick to what I said—it might look rather funny if I changed it now. (*He puts his drink on the stool*)

(EDWARD *sits in the armchair* LC. *There is a pause*)

(*He rises and mooches to the french windows*) What shall we do now, Edward? I'm bored. Would you like to go for a walk?

EDWARD. No, thank you. (*He pauses*) Please go on your own if you'd like to. (*He leans back and closes his eyes*)

MAURICE. No, not by myself. (*He holds the window curtain aside and stares out, his face pressed close to the pane. Urgently*) Edward!

EDWARD (*stirring*) Mm?

MAURICE (*more urgently*) Edward!

EDWARD (*sitting up*) Yes?

MAURICE. I can see a face in the trees—in the creeper.

EDWARD (*quietly*) Maurice—close the curtains.

(MAURICE *lets the curtains fall back*)

MAURICE (*turning and crossing to Edward*) I don't feel very well. I have a terrible headache.

EDWARD (*kindly*) Why don't you go and lie down?

MAURICE. No—no, I don't want to—I'm all right, really—it's just my head.

(*There is a pause*)

EDWARD. Why don't you go and take some aspirin?

MAURICE. It wouldn't do any good. It's not that kind of headache. We could go away from here for a bit, couldn't we, Edward? We could go to the Continent—or France—I'd like to go there.

(EDWARD *is silent*)

Once I wanted to go to France—with the school. They went for two days—I was the only boy in our form who didn't go. But we could go, we could go together, couldn't we, Edward?

EDWARD. Maurice—I don't know.

(*There is a pause*)

MAURICE (*picking up the cards*) You're worried about me, aren't you, Edward? You didn't eat any dinner because you were worried about me—but you don't have to worry about me because I'm perfectly all right. (*He flips the cards*) I'm more all right than a lot of people. (*He flips the cards*)

EDWARD. Please don't do that, Maurice. I've told you before, it spoils the cards.

MAURICE. Sorry. (*He spreads the cards into a fan, kneels in front of Edward and holds them out*) Tell my fortune.

(EDWARD *pushes the cards aside*)

Go on.

EDWARD (*quietly*) I can't tell fortunes, Maurice.

MAURICE. I want to see if you turn up the Queen of Spades. I think it's very exciting to turn up the Queen of Spades. (*He holds the cards out towards Edward*) Take a card.

(EDWARD *pushes Maurice's hand away and accidentally knocks the cards on to the floor*)

EDWARD. I'm not in the mood for games, Maurice.

MAURICE. All right. I'm sorry.

(EDWARD *rises and crosses up* RC)

Are you ill, Edward?

EDWARD. Yes, I suppose you might say I was ill.

MAURICE. Can I get you anything? Can I do anything for you? (*He rises, leaving the cards on the floor*)

EDWARD. Yes, Maurice. You can be quiet.

MAURICE. Oh. I'm sorry. You are funny, Edward. When I first came to this house I didn't have anything to say. But I do now, I talk to you. I thought you'd be glad when I talk.

EDWARD. You were not talking, Maurice—you were prattling.

(*He pauses*) If you really wanted to talk to me, I would be glad to listen.

MAURICE. Talk about what, Edward? (*He sits on the sofa*)

EDWARD. There is something you don't talk about, Maurice. If we could talk about that, perhaps I could help you. Maurice, there's something you don't seem able to understand. If you keep a terrible thing in your head and try to pretend it isn't there—it will grow and grow—and one day it will explode in your brain. Do you realize that?

(MAURICE *is silent*)

We pay for what we do, Maurice. If you deny to yourself what you have done, you might as well deny your own existence—because you will be condemned for ever to living outside yourself—living like the creeper on that tree in the garden. Living on the outside, until the underneath is dead.

(MAURICE *is silent*)

(*He crosses to Maurice*) Maurice, will you confide in me?

(*There is a pause*)

MAURICE. It sounds as if it's raining. I couldn't have gone for my walk, anyway.

(*The door bell rings*)

Who's that? (*He jumps up*) Who would that be?

EDWARD. I don't know. Holmes will answer the door. Why don't you sit down?

MAURICE (*sitting on the edge of the sofa*) It's late—terribly late. Who would come here at this hour? (*He takes out his cigarette case. His hand is shaking slightly*)

EDWARD (*his voice lowered*) You must keep calm.

(HOLMES *enters from the hall*)

HOLMES. A gentleman to see you, sir. The same gentleman who called once before, sir.

EDWARD. Show him in, Holmes. (*He stands with his back to the fire, his hands behind him*)

(HOLMES *exits to the hall*)

MAURICE (*rising*) I think I'll go upstairs.

(EDWARD *moves to Maurice and puts a restraining hand on his shoulder*)

EDWARD (*softly*) It's much better to stay where you are. Sit down.

(MAURICE *resumes his seat.*
HOLMES *enters from the hall and stands to one side.*

SCENE 2 — THE CREEPER

The MAN *enters from the hall. He is dressed as before in a white mackintosh*)

Good evening.

(HOLMES *exits to the hall, closing the door behind him.* MAURICE *rises*)

MAN. Good evening. (*To Maurice*) Don't get up, please.

(MAURICE *resumes his seat*)

I'm sorry to call on you so late, Mr Kimberley, but I happened to be in the district—and we're very busy, you know.

EDWARD (*pleasantly*) That's quite all right. Would you care for a drink?

MAN (*after the faintest hesitation*) Thank you, sir. It's a bit nippy out.

EDWARD (*moving to the sideboard*) Brandy? Or would you prefer something else?

MAN. No. That'll do me.

EDWARD (*pouring the brandy*) Water or soda?

MAN. Just as it is.

EDWARD. Splendid! The only way to drink it. (*He hands the drink to the* MAN) Maurice, will you have another?

MAURICE. Yes, please, Edward. (*Glad of an excuse, he rises and takes his glass to Edward*)

EDWARD (*to the* MAN) Please sit down. (*He indicates the sofa*)

MAN. Thank you. (*He sits on the sofa*)

EDWARD (*pouring a drink for Maurice*) Maurice.

(MAURICE *sits in the chair down* L)

(*To the* MAN) Well, what news of Mr Sanderson? (*He takes the drink to Maurice then stands up* LC)

MAN. None, I'm afraid, sir.

EDWARD. Oh, I was hoping that was why you called.

MAN. No, sir. I take it you've not had any communication, sir?

EDWARD. I'm afraid not. These friends of Michel, where he lodged—don't they have any idea what could have happened to him?

MAN. No, sir. He never returned there after his visit to you.

EDWARD. Does he owe them some money?

MAN. I believe he does, sir.

EDWARD. As I thought. They are not concerned so much about where he is, as about how much he owes them. Perhaps you would inform them I shall be happy to settle his debts.

MAN. There's no reason for you to do that, sir.

EDWARD. No reason whatever, but I shall do so just the same.

MAN. Mr Kimberley, am I correct in thinking that you gave Mr Sanderson a cheque the afternoon he came here for tea?

EDWARD. Perfectly correct.
MAURICE (*in a rather strained voice*) Edward, why . . .?
(EDWARD *and the* MAN *look at Maurice*)
(*He mumbles*) Sorry.
MAN. May I ask why you gave it?
EDWARD. I thought it would tide him over until he found a new position.
MAN. Mr Kimberley, did Mr Sanderson suggest you gave him some money?
EDWARD. Not at all. It was entirely voluntary.
MAN. Could you tell me if he has cashed that cheque?
EDWARD. I really don't have the least idea. However, you can get that information from my bank. You have my permission to do so.
MAN. Thank you, Mr Kimberley, it would be very helpful. If he cashed it—well, he could be anywhere. If he didn't—well, we may have to draw certain conclusions.
MAURICE (*quickly*) You mean suicide?
MAN. Possibly, Mr Morris, possibly.
EDWARD. Poor Michel—poor unhappy boy.
MAN (*putting his glass on the stool and rising*) Well, Mr Kimberley —Mr Morris, I hope I won't have to trouble you any further. Thank you both for your assistance. If you'll allow me, I should like to return your property. (*He takes a small box from his pocket with the eye in it*)

(EDWARD *lifts the lid of the silver box on the table* LC)

(*He places the eye in the box*) I'm sorry I had to do that, sir. I'm afraid in our job we have to sometimes take liberties—and you must admit it's rather a strange thing to find, sir.
EDWARD. Obviously my reputation as an eccentric has escaped you. (*He smiles*) And the blotting paper?
MAN (*smiling*) I didn't think you'd be needing that, sir. (*He pauses briefly*) Well, sir, I'll be getting along. Thank you both for your assistance.

(EDWARD *moves to the fireplace and rings the bell*)

EDWARD. Not at all. I hope there'll be some news soon—good news. Perhaps you'll keep me informed. I feel rather concerned— after all, he was once in my employ.
MAN. Yes, sir, I'll do that.
EDWARD. Are you sure you wouldn't care for another drink before you go?
MAN. No, sir, thank you very much. By the way, Mr Morris, I've been meaning to ask you—can you tell me where you were previously employed?

(HOLMES *enters from the hall*)

MAURICE (*after a pause*) Austin Reed's.
EDWARD. Holmes will show you out. Good night.
MAN. Good night, Mr Kimberley—Mr Morris.

(MAURICE *half rises.*
The MAN *exits to the hall.*
HOLMES *follows him off.* MAURICE *drops back into his chair. He and* EDWARD *are both waiting for the sound of the front door closing. It seems a long time. As it bangs shut a faint sigh of relief seems to escape from both of them.* MAURICE, *enormously relieved and confident by the Man's departure, jumps up*)

MAURICE (*excitedly*) Let's have a drink, Edward. (*He takes his glass to the sideboard and refills it*) Cheers! My headache's gone.
EDWARD. Good. (*He moves to the desk, sits and writes*)

(MAURICE *laughs. He walks lightheartedly about and then flicks the lid of the box with the eye open and shut*)

MAURICE (*relaxed*) Well, we got the eye back. (*He pauses and sits in the armchair* LC) Edward. I've always been meaning to ask you —where's the rest of that dog?
EDWARD (*quietly*) In the garden.
MAURICE (*slightly subdued*) Oh. (*More cheerfully*) You told me he was a St Bernard, didn't you?
EDWARD. Labrador.
MAURICE. What was his name?
EDWARD. 'Max.'
MAURICE. What did he die of?
EDWARD. He went mad.
MAURICE. Mad? A dog? A dog can't go mad.
EDWARD. There are mad dogs as well as mad people. Maurice. (*He opens his cheque book*)
MAURICE. And then what?

(EDWARD *looks enquiringly at Maurice*)

Then what happened to the dog?
EDWARD (*turning back to the desk*) I had to have him put down.
MAURICE. Because he was mad? You had him put down because you thought . . . How did you know he was? How did you know?
EDWARD. Because he savaged people. (*He fills in a cheque*)
MAURICE (*rising*) Perhaps it was you—not the dog—that was . . . (*He breaks off and sits on the sofa*)
EDWARD (*quietly*) Perhaps.
MAURICE (*after a pause*) I don't think that man'll come back again, do you? (*He pauses*) Edward, I said . . .
EDWARD. Yes, Maurice, I heard you.
MAURICE. What are you doing?

EDWARD. I'm writing something. (*He extracts the cheque, blots it, folds it over, rises and goes to Maurice, the cheque in his hand*) Maurice?
MAURICE. Yes, Edward?
EDWARD. I think you ought to leave this house.

(MAURICE *turns pale with shock*)

It's the only thing to do—you can't stay here.
MAURICE. You're telling me to go! (*He jumps up*) Why? You've no right to do that.
EDWARD. I have every right to do that. But I'm not telling you to go, Maurice—I'm asking you to.
MAURICE. But this is my house. I can't go, I'm having lessons on the piano—my teacher says I'm brilliant—I can't stop my lessons.
EDWARD. Maurice, I will see to it that you can have other lessons—somewhere else.
MAURICE. Somewhere else? Where else? Where would I go, what would I do, if I left here? I'd have to be a salesman again. Is that what you want me to do—be a salesman again?
EDWARD. No, I don't. I want you to take this cheque—(*he holds out the cheque*)——

(MAURICE *takes the cheque as if he does not really know what he is doing and does not look at it*)

—it's for quite a lot of money—and go away—right away—anywhere in the world you want—do anything you want. You can begin again, start your life afresh—you're young, you can do that.
MAURICE. Where, Edward, where would I do that?
EDWARD. You could go to Venice—it's one of the most beautiful places in the world.
MAURICE (*like a small boy*) But I couldn't—I couldn't go by myself—I'd get lost.
EDWARD. You know—sometimes, to get lost, can be a very pleasant thing.
MAURICE (*sadly*) Come with me, Edward.
EDWARD. No, Maurice—you must go alone—and you must never return.
MAURICE. You want to be rid of me, don't you?
EDWARD. Don't be foolish, Maurice.
MAURICE. Yes, you do. You're sick of me, I know you're sick of me.
EDWARD. Maurice—please. I don't want you to go, it's for your own sake.
MAURICE (*defiantly*) Why, Edward? Why? What have I done?
EDWARD. Yes, Maurice—what have you done? (*He looks at Maurice*)

(MAURICE *holds* EDWARD's *gaze for a moment then breaks it and turns away*)

MAURICE (*still defiant*) Can I have a drink, please?

EDWARD (*gently*) Of course.

(MAURICE *goes to the sideboard, pours a brandy and drinks it nearly all in one go. He does not look at Edward*)

MAURICE. Who will you have in my place, Edward—have you advertised? What sort of a companion will you have now?

EDWARD (*quietly*) When you go, Maurice, there won't be anyone else.

(MAURICE *looks at Edward then crosses to the french windows, moves the curtain slightly and looks out at the creeper*)

MAURICE (*in a funny voice*) I don't believe you, Edward. You're just as lonely as I am.

(EDWARD *is silent*)

You were my friend. And you were my father, too. (*He pauses*) What would you do, Edward, if I didn't go?

EDWARD. Nothing—but it would make me very unhappy.

(*There is a pause then* MAURICE *turns and looks at Edward*)

MAURICE. I don't want to make you unhappy, Edward. (*He pauses briefly*) I love you.

(MAURICE *and* EDWARD *look at each other for a moment then* MAURICE *crosses and exits to the hall.* EDWARD *looks at the closed door for a moment, goes slowly to the fireplace, rings the bell then crosses to the french windows. There is a pause.*

HOLMES *enters from the hall, moves* LC *and collects the cards from the floor.* EDWARD *moves the curtains aside a little and gazes out of the window*)

EDWARD (*in a strained sort of voice*) It's raining.

HOLMES (*quietly*) Yes, sir.

(*There is a pause*)

EDWARD. You know, Holmes, I'm afraid if we have a storm the tree will come down.

HOLMES. That tree will survive us, sir.

EDWARD. Do you think so? (*He pauses*) It's strange to be so attached to a dead thing—but you know, Holmes, I feel as if the whole of my life was in that tree. I look at it and I see a hundred faces—and all are mine.

(*There is a pause.* HOLMES *puts the cards on the desk*)

Do you remember when I used to climb it as a little boy?

HOLMES. Yes, sir. I was the only one who knew where to find you.

EDWARD (*with a mocking laugh*) I used to hide from the women. (*He turns and moves* C) Ah, well, that was a long time ago.

(*There is a pause.* HOLMES *goes to the fire and puts a log on*)
(*His voice changes*) Holmes.
  HOLMES. Yes, sir?
  EDWARD. Holmes—would you take a glass of brandy with me? I would be very happy if you would.
  HOLMES. Yes, sir, it would give me great pleasure.
  (*They look at each other with understanding*)
Would you like me to pour the brandy, sir?
  EDWARD (*crossing to the sideboard*) No, Holmes—allow me to pour it for you. (*He pours a brandy for Holmes, refills his own glass and hands Holmes his drink*)
  HOLMES. Thank you, sir.
  EDWARD. No, Holmes, it is I who should thank you. (*He lifts his glass*)
  (*They silently toast one another and drink*)
Fifty years you have looked after me, Holmes—fifty years.
  HOLMES. Yes, sir.
  EDWARD (*after a pause*) It's strange, isn't it, Holmes—that the only things we have ever said to each other in fifty years have been—in terms of speech—a few meaningless courtesies.
  HOLMES (*nodding*) Yes, sir.
  (*There is a pause*)
(*He clears his throat*) I once took a brandy with your father, sir—just the once in his lifetime. I always remember it.
  EDWARD (*smiling*) And now you take one in mine.
  (*There is a pause. They drink*)
Holmes—I want to tell you, that I have asked Mr Morris to leave this house.
  HOLMES. Yes, sir.
  EDWARD. I gave him a substantial sum of money and told him to go abroad and try to begin his life again. Do you think I was wrong?
  HOLMES. No, sir, I don't think you were wrong. He shouldn't stay in this house, sir.
  EDWARD. Only you and I, Holmes. You and I are part of this house and we shall never leave it.
  HOLMES. No, sir. (*He puts his glass on the sideboard*)
  EDWARD. You must go to bed now, Holmes, and thank you.
  HOLMES. Thank *you*, sir.
  EDWARD. Good night, Holmes.
  HOLMES. Good night, sir. (*He moves slowly to the hall door*)
  (EDWARD *moves to the desk and switches off the desk lamp, then turns to* Holmes)

SCENE 2 THE CREEPER

EDWARD. Holmes.
HOLMES (*stopping and turning*) Yes, sir?
EDWARD. You will look after the garden, won't you?
HOLMES. Yes, sir.

HOLMES, *slowly and bent, exits to the hall and closes the door behind him.* EDWARD *crosses to* R, *switches out the table-lamp* R, *looks at his hands then pulls the curtains aside and gazes out of the french windows.*

MAURICE *enters silently from the hall. His silhouette appears as if from nowhere, a band of feathers round his head and a bow and arrow in his hands. Slowly the silhouette raises the bow and arrow and takes aim. We see the bow-string pulled back and we hear the soft 'ping'. An arrow sinks into the small of Edward's back. Slowly* EDWARD's *body crumples. His hands slither down the velvet curtains, slowly, slowly, until he reaches the floor. The black shadow vanishes.* EDWARD *lies still, crumpled on the floor, the arrow sticking out of his back. The sound of* MAURICE *playing Beethoven's 'Für Elise' on the piano is heard as—*

the CURTAIN *falls*

AUTHOR'S NOTES

Whether or not the tree is part of the setting is optional. Unless it were a good tree, it might be better if it were in one's imagination.

At the start of each scene, all french windows are closed except the downstage half of the middle window which remains open throughout.

Music—for Edward and Maurice on the piano—Beethoven's *Für Elise*

Music—from radio for Edward—from *Les Sylphides*

Music—from radio for Michel—*Where did our Love Go?* (The Supremes)

FURNITURE AND PROPERTY LIST

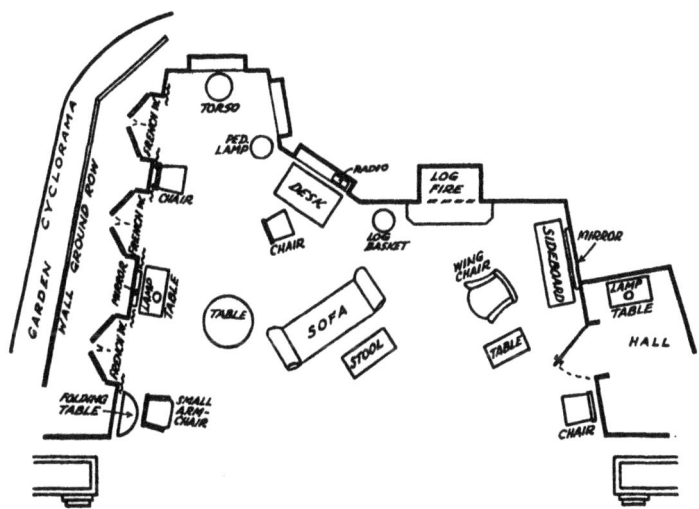

ACT I
Scene 1

On stage—Folding-table (down R). *On it:* bowl with fruit, including grapes, 2 packs of cards
    On wall down R: picture
    Small armchair (down R)
    Table (R). *On it:* silver cigarette box with cigarettes, matches in silver matchbox holder, ashtray, table-lamp
    On wall over table R: mirror
    Occasional chair (up R)
    Torso and stand (up R)
    Pedestal (up R). *On it:* lamp
    Desk. *On it:* pen and ink stand, correspondence, blotter pad, blotting paper, stationery holder with stationery, cheque book, carafe of water, glass, pill bottle, ornamental dressing
        In drawer: gold cigarette lighter in box
    Built-in bookshelves (in alcove). *In them:* books
    Desk chair
    Built-in radio
    Log basket. *In it:* logs
    Log firegrate
    Fire dogs
    Bell-pull (R of fireplace)
    Over mantelpiece: large portrait of female
    On mantelpiece: ornamental dressing
    Sideboard. *On it:* table-lamp, tantalus, silver tray with 8 brandy glasses, ornamental dressing

On wall over sideboard: mirror
Occasional chair (down L)
Small round table (RC). *On it:* cake plate with petit-fours
Empire style sofa. *On it:* cushions
Stool. *On it:* ashtray
Wing chair (LC)
Occasional table (LC). *On it:* ornate box with eye in plastic holder,
　　　　　　　　　　　　ashtray
On floor LC: letter
2 chandeliers
On floor LC: circular carpet
Light switches below door L
Rectangular carpet RC
Velvet window curtains
In hall: hall table. *On it:* lamp
　　　　　On wall: picture

Door open
All french windows closed except downstage half of middle window
Fire on
Fittings off
Window curtains open

Off stage—Silver tray. *On it:* pot of tea, 3 cups, 3 saucers, 3 teaspoons, cream
　　　　　　　　jug, sugar bowl with lump sugar and tongs, small dish
　　　　　　　　with lemon slices (MICHEL)

Personal—MAURICE: watch, envelope
　　　　　　EDWARD: gold cigarette case with cigarettes, gold lighter, watch
　　　　　　MICHEL: handkerchief

SCENE 2

Strike—Tea tray and tea things
Set—*On Stool* LC: tray with 2 glasses of hot milk, bottle of old brandy, 2 brandy
　　　　　　glasses
Chandeliers lit
Window curtains closed
Door open
French windows closed
Fire on

Off stage—Tartan rug (EDWARD)
　　　　　　Tea-cloth (HOLMES)

Personal—EDWARD: spectacles
　　　　　　MAURICE: balloon, string, wallet. *In it:* £1 note
　　　　　　MICHEL: watch

ACT II
SCENE 1

Strike—Wet carpet
　　　　Rug
　　　　Plate of petit-fours
　　　　Bowl of fruit
　　　　Cards
　　　　Balloon and string from fireplace

Set—*On sideboard:* clean brandy glasses
　　　Dry duplicate carpet RC
　　　On stool: copy of *The Times*
　　　On table RC: ashtray

THE CREEPER 61

In alcove up R: jig-saw on stand, partly done
On chair up R: jig-saw box with pieces
Re-set chairs down R and up R
Transfer cigarette box from table R to table RC
Fittings off
Window curtains open
Fire on
Door closed
Downstage half of middle french window open

Off stage—Bow, quiver and arrows (MAURICE)
     Red Indian brave feather head-band (MAURICE)
     Bow, quiver and arrows (EDWARD)
     Red Indian Chief feather head-dress (EDWARD)
     Tray. *On it:* bottle of Campari, 2 glasses, soda syphon in holder, ice
      bucket with ice and tongs (HOLMES)

Personal—EDWARD: small pin-up cutting, silk handkerchief, cigarette case with
    cigarettes, lighter
    MAURICE: wallet. *In it:* £1 note, creased papers, N.H.S. card, small
     photographs

SCENE 2

Strike: Copy of *The Times*
  Drinks tray and glasses
Set—*On stool* LC: ashtray, box with cigarettes
Fittings off
Window curtains open
Fire on
Door closed
French windows closed

Off stage—Tray. *On it:* pot of tea, 3 cups, 3 saucers, 3 teaspoons, cream jug,
    bowl of lump sugar with tongs (HOLMES)
   Plate of cakes (HOLMES)

Personal—MICHEL: empty cigarette packet
    MAURICE: packet of cigarettes, gold lighter
    EDWARD: case with cigarettes, lighter

ACT III
SCENE 1

Strike—Tray and tea things
  Jig-saw and stand
  Jig-saw box
  Ashtray from stool
  Wallet and photographs from fire
Set—*In alcove:* table with train unit

Fittings off
Window curtains open
Fire on
Door closed
Middle section of french window open

Off stage—Silver salver. *On it:* visiting card (HOLMES)
   Parcels (MAURICE)

Personal—MAURICE: gold cigarette case with cigarettes, lighter
    MAN: notebook, pencil, identity-card case, handkerchief
    EDWARD: cigarette case with cigarettes, lighter

SCENE 2

Strike—Dirty glass
    Parcels
    Maurice's coat

Set—*On stool:* playing cards
Chandeliers lit
Window curtains closed
Door closed
French windows closed
Fire on

Off stage—Feather head-band, bow, arrow (MAURICE)

Personal—MAURICE: cigarette case
        MAN: box with eye

LIGHTING PLOT

Property Fittings Required—2 chandeliers, 4 table-lamps, log fire
Interior. A lounge. The same scene throughout. Hall

 THE APPARENT SOURCES OF LIGHT ARE—in daytime, french windows R, and at night, chandeliers up RC and down LC, and table-lamps R, up RC, L and in the hall L

 THE MAIN ACTING AREAS ARE—up RC, down RC, C, and LC

ACT I SCENE 1 Afternoon

To open: Effect of afternoon sunshine
    Fittings off
    Fire on

Cue	1	MICHEL: 'Dance with me?' *Slow dim of general lighting for dusk effect*	(page 11)
Cue	2	At end of Scene BLACK-OUT	(page 12)

ACT I SCENE 2 Night

To open: Chandeliers on
    Fire on
    Dark outside windows

Cue	3	EDWARD switches on desk lamp *Snap in desk lamp*	(page 16)
Cue	4	EDWARD switches out desk lamp *Snap out desk lamp*	(page 17)
Cue	5	EDWARD switches out chandeliers *Snap out chandeliers* *Snap out covering lights*	(page 17)
Cue	6	MICHEL switches on lamp L *Snap on lamp L* *Snap on covering lights*	(page 17)
Cue	7	HOLMES switches on chandeliers *Snap in chandeliers* *Snap in covering lights*	(page 21)

ACT II SCENE 1 Morning

To open: Effect of morning sunshine
    Fittings off
    Fire on

Cue	8	At end of Scene BLACK-OUT	(page 31)

ACT II SCENE 2 Afternoon

To open: Effect of sunset
    Fittings off
    Fire on

Cue	9	After start of Scene *Commence slow dim of lights for dusk effect*	(page 32)

Cue 10	HOLMES switches on chandeliers *Snap in chandeliers* *Snap in covering lights*	(page 34)

ACT III SCENE 1 Midday

To open: Effect of sunshine
    Fittings off
    Fire on

Cue 11	At end of Scene BLACK-OUT	(page 47)

ACT III SCENE 2 Night

To open: Table-lamps on
    Chandeliers off
    Fire on
    Dark outside windows

Cue 12	EDWARD switches off desk lamp *Snap out desk lamp* *Snap out covering lights*	(page 56)
Cue 13	EDWARD switches off lamp R *Snap out lamp* R *Snap out covering lights*	(page 57)

EFFECTS PLOT

ACT I
Scene 1

Cue	1	EDWARD switches on radio *Ballet music*	(page 4)
Cue	2	EDWARD switches off radio *Stop music*	(page 4)
Cue	3	MICHEL switches on radio *Hot jazz music*	(page 11)
Cue	4	Follows above cue *Knocking from upstairs*	(page 11)
Cue	5	MICHEL adjusts radio *Increase volume of music*	(page 11)
Cue	6	EDWARD switches off radio *Stop music*	(page 11)
Cue	7	MICHEL exits *Front door slams*	(page 11)

Scene 2

Cue	8	At start of Scene *Sound of classical piano music*	(page 12)
Cue	9	HOLMES attends to the fire *Stop piano music*	(page 12)

ACT II
Scene 1

No cues

Scene 2

No cues

ACT III
Scene 1

Cue	10	EDWARD: '... very close thing.' *Door bell rings*	(page 40)

Scene 2

Cue	11	MAURICE: '... my walk, anyway.' *Door bell rings*	(page 50)
Cue	12	The MAN and HOLMES exit *Front door slams*	(page 53)
Cue	13	At end of Scene *Sound of piano playing Beethoven's 'Für Elise'*	(page 57)

www.ingramcontent.com/pod-product-compliance
Ingram Content Group UK Ltd.
Pitfield, Milton Keynes, MK11 3LW, UK
UKHW021847210426
5322IPUK00022B/508